Contents

Currency Press acknowledges the Traditional Owners of the Country on which we live and work. We pay our respects to all Aboriginal and Torres Strait Islander Elders, past and present.

For Lucy

I'M WITH HER

VICTORIA MIDWINTER PITT

CURRENCY PRESS
The performing arts publisher

CURRENCY PLAYS

First published in 2022
by Currency Press Pty Ltd,
PO Box 2287, Strawberry Hills, NSW, 2012, Australia
enquiries@currency.com.au
www.currency.com.au

The author and publisher have made every reasonable effort to identify the copyright holders for the images used. If anyone has any queries, please contact the publisher at the above address.

Typeset by Brighton Gray for Currency Press.
Cover design by Alissa Dinallo for Currency Press.

A catalogue record for this book is available from the National Library of Australia

Introduction

There are moments in history when the forces of what have come before and the energy of the present reconfigure the social and political landscape. *I'm With Her* burns with the generational energy of its characters, young and old, who believe in the potential for transformation toward a world capable of embracing, and not violently undermining, women and girls.

In Australia, and around the globe, reckoning with misogyny and the interrelated issues of systemic racism and patriarchal destruction has been centuries in the making. These are not issues that have come from nowhere, presenting themselves now because the time is right. As *I'm With Her* states through the poignant lines of the environmental scientist Marion Blackwell, 'Time's got nothing to do with growth ... time doesn't do the work'. It is women, of all backgrounds, throughout history, who do the work—who keep families together, communities functioning and economies circulating. It is women's work that makes growth happen.

The stories throughout *I'm With Her* show how living as women and girls, and having dreams that do not fit gender norms, are themselves acts of resistance against dominant sexist systems and behaviours.

Change happens, misogyny is called out and confronted over and again because of women's voices and actions. Victoria Midwinter Pitt's play play reminds us—all women—of how much power we have in being ourselves. But to be all of who we are, without trepidation, in a world that condemns so much of our diverse womanhood is often the hardest thing to do. There is a moment in the play where all the characters sing out the repetitive self-deprecating lines that are all too common for so many women: 'Why am I doing this? ... Am I shit? ... God I must be shit.' The truth is this internal voice that takes away our self-worth and power is not ours—it's the gendered shaming and violence of patriarchy.

I'm With Her triumphs over this false voice in reasserting the real voices of women, proving that we are never only victims. We are survivors, activists, trailblazers, negotiators, carers, leaders—the list of our attributes and successes is endless. This play uses the real-life stories of its extraordinary characters to always rise up beyond supposed defeat or crisis.

The women here—the bartender, the prime minister, the sex worker and the academic, to name just a few—refuse to accept that this current reality is good enough. When abused, told and shown that this world isn't for them they do the most courageous thing of continuing to be themselves, of occupying space and pursuing their interests. They do not sit down or move to the side, and they are certainly not silent. Because of that, in their own ways, each woman challenges the status quo, changes the narrative, and begins to carve out a different reality.

This theme of resistance and finding strength in identity, threaded throughout the play, reminds me of the women who raised me—my matriarchal lineage. My grandmother, a Bunuba woman, was born at the turn of the last century, in the rocky ranges, freshwater springs and grassy plains of the central Kimberley, in the far north of Western Australia. In the aftermath of a brutal colonial onslaught, she never relinquished her Bunuba knowledge and ways of being and living on our traditional Country.

She was always distrusting of the white man's laws and ways of learning, and she stopped my mother from going to school, saying to her, 'I will teach you everything you need to know'. My mother learnt how to live within our Country in reciprocal relationship with our non-human relatives, as thousands of generations of girls before her had done. I was brought up across two worlds—the Western and Bunuba. My grandmother's and mother's determination meant that our knowledge, stretching back to time immemorial, survived. Because of them I could navigate a Western reality while also remaining strong in my Bunuba womanhood.

I will always be eternally grateful for these women who stood on the precipice of the frontier, marched forward into a new world, and brought our society, culture and ways of being with them. The pain and horrors they lived through to do that are indescribable.

Australia is etched with the stories and wisdom of First Nations women like my mother and grandmother. These are women whose names won't be remembered in the history books. Women who turned the soils with their digging sticks, nursed children, healed the sick, sang and danced for rain and food, governed societies, ensured everyone was fed while the environment was cyclically replenished. As the first mothers to walk this continent they formed the right conditions for Australian ecosystems, which included humanity, to thrive and sustain the oldest living civilizations on earth.

We know some of the names of women who fought fiercely to protect this precious existence from devastation, like Barangaroo and Truganini. There would be hundreds, thousands more. I'm sure they knew, as women do, that their fight was worth it because today, our First Nations women and cultures live on. And now, in this contemporary moment, it's the voices of women such as Marcia Langton, heard throughout *I'm With Her*, which will ensure that Australians everywhere are educated in and come to celebrate our incredible living heritage of First Nations matriarchal leadership and knowledges. As Marcia's character states in the play: 'Other women can learn a lot from Aboriginal women.' We still have a long way to go, but all the women I know are taking us toward the future we want.

As the first woman to become the Aboriginal and Torres Strait Islander Social Justice Commissioner, in the role's 25-year history, I was also determined to be a part of changing the narrative. At the beginning of my term, I launched the multi-year Wiyi Yani U Thangani project, meaning Women's Voices in Bunuba. Throughout 2018, my team and I traversed Australia, travelling to over 100 urban and remote communities to elevate and make visible the diverse lives and work of our First Nations women and girls. It was the first time since 1986 that First Nations women and girls had been heard as a collective. It resulted in a once in a generation report that will be used as the roadmap for achieving First Nations gender justice and equality at the first ever Aboriginal and Torres Strait Islander women and girls' national summit in 2023.

Wiyi Yani U Thangani conclusively shows how—despite their absences from the arenas of decision-making due to ongoing structural marginalisation—our women are present across all of life. Our women carry knowledge about sustaining existence and are doing the backbone work of society—caring for children, family and Country—and are at the forefront of driving economic and social change. Wiyi Yani U Thangani describes how when First Nations women are in the driving seat of life, harms are reduced, children thrive, economies grow, and more equitable and sustainable ways of organizing society are introduced. Advancing the gender justice of First Nations women is clearly in the interests of all Australians—First Nations and non-Indigenous women and girls, men, and boys.

First and foremost, Wiyi Yani U Thangani belongs to all First Nations women and girls. But it is also a generous invitation to all Australians to come on the journey with us in creating a more equitable and vibrant Australian society.

I'm With Her makes it clear that the society we have a right to— that treats women and girls with respect, that calls out and proactively eradicates all forms of discrimination, that honours women's knowledges and creates structures informed by them—is yet to exist. *I'm With Her,* like Wiyi Yani U Thangani, reminds us that we should not wait for it to arrive, but that it is within our actions, every day, that we bring the world we want into being.

I feel the impatience of the characters in the play, and I know all the women I've spoken to throughout Wiyi Yani U Thangani feel it too— that we will not sit down or stand to the side until we are responded to and the world around us begins to shake and shift. In reflecting on the words of Julie Bates, while there are still laws and structures that harm us, I cannot rest. I know that our rights and our First Nations Laws must be reinscribed into this vast continent for Australian society, our collective spirit as a nation to become whole and healthy.

I too, like the women in this play, am dreaming of myself as a young girl. I am staring up into the eyes of my grandmother; beside her, my mother stands tall, looking out to the horizon. Our feet are bare and warm in the pindan soils of our Country. I clasp my grandmother's hand and look around; gathered are our peoples and hundreds of other women from every part of the word. Slowly, they take their shoes off and dig their toes and heels into the earth, and say in unison, 'We are ready, we are listening, we are here to learn'. Then there is a deafening silence before the hum of the earth fills our ears.

The publication of *I'm With Her* comes as the public is hearing the rising tide of women's voices once again, propelled by frustration, fury, love and determination. The #MeToo movement has had a full throttle resurgence in Australia, and these dreams, of all our women, feel that much more real each day.

June Oscar AO
Aboriginal and Torres Strait Islander Social Justice Commissioner
January 2022

Writer's Note

1.

This play is a conversation.

The first draft was made in 2019. The idea was to create a play from Australian women's accounts of their #MeToo experiences, with a focus on that part of the story we often leave out—the opposition, the resistance women mount and have always mounted to this shit. There is vital—and dangerous—information in that part of our stories. I wanted to find out how it might change our sense of both ourselves and what could happen next, if we pulled at that golden thread.

I began by just speaking with women from all over the country. Everyone had a story to tell. But in 2019—before names like Grace Tame and Brittany Higgins had erupted into our headlines and catalysed Australia's biggest #MeToo reckoning—very few women wanted to tell their story publicly.

But those first months of absorbing so many different stories were still invaluable—the little details of memory, the big realisations, the sweep of emotions I heard, added up to a shape that began to impress itself into me, a kind of map.

2.

The women who agreed to give their own story to this script, Nikki Keating, Julie Bates, Patricia Madigan, Pam Burridge, Julia Gillard, Marcia Langton, Marion Blackwell and Anne Aly are very different women. For all their differences, they are in no way intended to represent a cross section of Australian women. They represent only themselves. Their experience is unique. And at the same time there are things about the story each of them tells that so many women and girls will relate to.

Across about five months I spoke with each of them in a series of long, free-flowing, intimate conversations. Sometimes when I heard echoes in the predicaments they described, I'd share pieces of their stories across the group, and carry back fascinating responses.

The act of *listening* took on a particular force in this process. What I was hearing, in a way I had not heard before, was my own story. As a documentary filmmaker, I've spent my working life holding the space for intimate conversations, but for the first time the experience I was asking others to describe was one I fundamentally shared. It changed the way I worked: I found myself joining in, taking new risks, pushing boundaries. And being pushed. My contributors and I stretched each other with the questions we knew to ask each other. We surprised, sometimes shocked, ourselves with our answers.

Julia Gillard's monologue involved a different process from the rest, but one still rooted in conversation. I first met Julia Gillard when I interviewed her for the documentary *Afghanistan: Inside Australia's War*. For *I'm With Her*, I took my starting point from something she had said to me—that the one thing everyone wanted her to speak about was her famous misogyny speech and perhaps Australian women were missing a larger point she'd been trying to make about her prime ministership. Instead of another interview, we agreed I would work with the words she'd already put on the public record to create a monologue that threw down the challenge of a re-focus. And this process too was shared and shaped with the wider group.

Over the months, organically, eight conversations grew into one conversation across the group. That dynamic is the spiritual foundation of the show.

Then, by a long, winding process that was part epic spreadsheet and part deep instinct, I began to build a play from the raw mountain of words they'd given me. I wanted to distill into two hours a direct experience for the audience of our conversations, individual, and collective. Dramaturg Francesca Smith was a wise and brilliant player in this process—asking questions and opening space for discoveries.

Each woman worked closely with me in refining and approving the final text of their monologues. Julia Gillard gave her consent for the use of her words, but offered no comment nor asked for any revisions.

These are their stories. Told to and shaped by me. Finished by us together. Owned and given to you, by them.

3.

I'm indebted to the cast of the original production at the Eternity Playhouse in Sydney 2019—Emily Havea, Lynette Curran, Gabrielle Chan, Shakira Clanton and Deborah Galanos—for standing the show up in the spirit it was made.

The script for that first production was rough, but the power of the stories burned through. And every one of those performers had her own story too and these inevitably co-mingled and multiplied the stories we were telling.

But what we bet on, and what we found out, was that the real juggernaut of this piece is actually not on stage. It's the audience. You couldn't write or act what the audience has got to give this show—the sheer mass of intelligent empathetic listening, absorbing these stories, recognising themselves in them and (even in silence) pouring out their own experience in reply. Given real space, *listened* to, the audience will create the raw feeling and the dynamism of the show.

The keys to this are simple but they require courage from those on stage. Look the audience in the eye. Talk to them. Know what the audience—statistically, on a theory of probabilities (to borrow from Marcia Langton)—has carried from their own lives into the theatre with them. Find the moments to slow down and hear what is actually unfolding in the room. From Nikki Keating's first anecdote of her mother pulling at her skirt, to Anne Aly's final raging call to arms, have the experience of these stories *with* the audience, not on their behalf.

4.

After the original Eternity Playhouse season, the script has been developed and refined, again with the close collaboration of the contributors and dramaturg Francesca Smith, and I would say the play is complete, but I have a feeling and a wish that it may evolve again.

To test our work, a little army of friends and family packed my kitchen for two staged readings of the play. None of the readers who delivered the script from around the kitchen table were professional actors, just smart, sparky women—they gave us two fantastic shows. I hope *I'm With Her* plays on big stages to big audiences, and I hope just as fervently that all sorts of groups of women and girls (and boys and men) will pick it up and stage intimate readings of it like this.

This is the task I now hand over to anyone who stands up to perform or read this play. Hear your own story as you talk to us. Listen to us listening. The conversation is not finished. We're just getting started. Find out what happens next.

Victoria Midwinter Pitt
January 2022

Acknowledgements

I'm With Her was developed with the support of the West Australian Government through the Department of Local Government, Sport and Cultural Industries Arts as part of the U-15K programme and the Fremantle Arts Centre through its Artist in Residence programme.

Thanks also to:
Dramaturg Francesca Smith—so smart, and so kind.

And to:
The original cast and crew of the 2019 production, and to Sophie Blacklaw, Lilly Powell, Sarah Gilbert, Chrys Stevenson, Marion Stell, Michele Lee, Arielle Cottingham, Jordan Raskopoulus, Maeve Marsden, Libby Wood, Rick and Sonia Rifici, Ben Broady, Bryant Apolonio and Jacob Van Der Walle from the Australian Writers Guild, Suzie Miller, Elena Macrides, Stephanie Faulkner, Claire Grady and Katie Pollock and all at Currency Press, Penny Chapman, Bruce Belsham, Wendy Beckett, Justin di Lollo, Bruce Wolpe, Connie Blefari, Roanna McClelland, Andrew Arestides, Georgia Richter, Wendy Martin, Tracy Routledge, Sarah Pearce, Deborah May, Lucy Griffiths, Ra Stewart, Anne-Louise Willoughby, Valerie Midwinter Pitt, Paola Anselmi, Fiona Leiper, Priya Wilson, Martin Pitt, June Oscar AO and Erin Phillips.

Deep thanks to all the women who told me their stories in the making of this script.

Department of
Local Government, Sport
and Cultural Industries
GOVERNMENT OF
WESTERN AUSTRALIA

City of
Fremantle

FREMANTLE
ARTS CENTRE

I'm With Her was first produced by Darlinghurst Theatre Company at the Eternity Playhouse, Sydney, on 9 November 2019, with the following cast:

Emily Havea
Lynette Curran
Gabrielle Chan
Shakira Clanton
Deborah Galanos

Director, Victoria Midwinter Pitt
Dramaturg, Francesca Smith
Designer, Mia Holton
Lighting Designer, Kelsey Lee
Sound Designer and Composer, Tegan Nicholls
Stage Manager, Amy Morcom
Production Manager, Lila Neiswanger

Original concept by Darlinghurst Theatre Company. Concept by Victoria Midwinter Pitt.

CHARACTERS

ACT ONE: THE ELEPHANT IN THE ROOM

Prologue:	Seeds, Waking
Woman 1	Nikki Keating
Woman 2	Julie Bates
Woman 3	Patricia Madigan
Woman 4	Pam Burridge
Woman 5	Julia Gillard

ACT TWO: THROWING THE ELEPHANT

Woman 6	Marcia Langton
Woman 7	Marion Blackwell
Woman 8	Anne Aly
Epilogue:	The Persistence of Dreams

NOTES

I'm With Her is a piece for eight performers. The original production involved some doubling of roles. A full eight-member cast is the best embodiment of the play and strongly recommended. The structure of the five monologues of Act One and three of Act Two should be maintained. The play makes use of projection for text and images. For simpler stagings, projections can be read out loud. Projections can be downloaded at www.imwithhertheplay.com

ACT ONE: THE ELEPHANT IN THE ROOM

PROLOGUE

Eight white stools in a broad semi-circle on a bare stage, white back and side walls. Text and images are projected onto this backdrop throughout the play.

Eight women enter and stand.

1.

WOMAN 7: When I was little I loved getting up and just going out into the bush. You'd fill your back-sack with oranges and out you'd go.

This was 1934, right up high in the Great Dividing Ranges. Formidable country. Very steep and scrubby. No straight paths—all scrambling and climbing.

You had to be *observant*, to know how to get home. There's a shape to all the stillness and movement.

It's an *ecosystem*. Every single bit, connected. It's innate to your being to understand how it functions.

Slow it down, let all the living pieces come apart.

2.

WOMAN 6: Selma, Alabama, 2006. A woman named Tarana Burke begins a movement to connect with other survivors of sexual abuse, most of them young women of colour. She frames her movement as a call:

PROJECTION: Me Too

WOMAN 5: Hollywood, 2017. Some of the most famous women in the world step forward to expose the harassment and abuse they've endured.

WOMAN 1: As the world struggles to understand—

WOMAN 8: How can this have gone on so long?

WOMAN 3: Why didn't someone say something?

WOMAN 5: Why didn't someone do something?

WOMAN 1: —those women pick up Tarana Burke's call.

WOMAN 4: In a day, from all over the world, five million of us answer:

ENSEMBLE: Me Too.

WOMAN 2: In the days and years that follow millions more of us tell our story.

WOMAN 8: Like little dots joining up to make a picture.

WOMAN 3: The impulse, once it gets going, is not easily turned off.

WOMAN 8: The picture does not come to stillness; it *spreads* …

WOMAN 1: … in so many directions …

WOMAN 3: … with so many questions …

WOMAN 1: … about what women are actually living with.

WOMAN 4: We are here to join that conversation.

WOMAN 6: We are here, on land where women have kept and carried stories for tens of thousands of years …

WOMAN 2: … to tell the stories of eight women,

WOMAN 6: And to hear together, the questions all our stories carry …

WOMAN 4: Is this ever going to change?

WOMAN 5: Is this just the way things are?

WOMAN 8: Do we *accept* this?

WOMAN 6: Do we?

>   *Pause.*

WOMAN 7: Slow it down, pull it apart.
>   Observe.
>   Some parts are dying, and fighting not to die.
>   Other parts are coming to new life.
>   Deep in the dirt.
>   Sit.
>   *They sit.*

Listen.

>   *Pause. Hearing the sound of the room.*

>   [*Looking out across the audience*] Seeds. Waking.

>   **PROJECTION: I'M WITH HER**

NIKKI KEATING

Nikki Keating performed by WOMAN 1.

1.

NIKKI KEATING: Growing up, I didn't know what I wanted to be. The very loud, very excitable child.

Maybe an actor?

I kind of wanted to be heard. I knew I wanted to be heard.

She stands.

I was ten when I got my period for the first time.

At school, all the girls around me were little girls, but by eleven, I had a woman's body.

It was like being given a box of jigsaw pieces but not the cover of the box. You have no idea what it is you're making.

I remember once my Mum tapping at me, pulling my dress down. A man was watching me.

It was super confusing.

Something beautiful. Something wrong.

PROJECTION: Nikki Keating

Born Brisbane, 1994

Bartender

2.

NIKKI KEATING: On my résumé, it says bartender and then it lists my skills. Wine and cocktails, kegs and stock, audio and lights, first aid.

What doesn't get listed and what anyone working in hospitality will surely understand, is what we're actually dealing with.

There are all of these tiny little—how you would describe it?— all these moments that happen throughout the night. Most people come to a bar outside the nine to five, when the rest of the city clocks off. It's the place everyone comes to celebrate and to commiserate, and as the night goes on things just get a bit more loose and real.

I was eighteen when I first started working in bars. It looked like fun. I could drink! It seemed smart to me.

Some jobs I got on these [*pointing*], the basics: my Large Breasts. At the time, I absolutely thought I was being hired on merit. Hilarious. Looking back, no. No no no no no.

First thing I learnt—in every bar there's a dress code. For the guys it's all wear the same thing—good jeans, collared shirts. For the girls—and look, I've got no problem with showing skin—for girls, the uniform is basically tight enough so you can see my body. But [*wry laugh*] not so tight I can't bend and lift a keg.

By eighteen we're used to being looked at and commented on.

But what I couldn't understand, was being touched.

3.

NIKKI KEATING: [*at a clip, not too heavy*] Like one time, it was an after party of a wedding. I'm carrying a tray full of drinks and there's music playing. And this guy walks up to me in front of everyone and just drums on my breasts!

Another time, it was a bucks' party. I was sent to take their orders, this group of eighteen, twenty men, all standing around me. And suddenly, the guy next to me takes my face in his hands, and licks me—right across my face!

Just tried to ignore it. Keep it light. Not make it worse.

4.

NIKKI KEATING: So then I'm nineteen, I'm working in a German restaurant, and I have to wear the most embarrassing version of a dirndl you've ever seen. Like about seventy percent of my breasts are out. And this was a 'family restaurant'.

This one night—really busy Friday night, I'm picking up cocktails off the main bar. And I feel someone's fist push against my back and wedge me against the bar. I'm just like, fuck—don't spill the drinks. I was shocked. I was confused.

Like everything was going on and I—
I didn't react.

Pause.

I took the drinks to the table.

I'm extremely grateful for what happened next—it was the guys I worked with who stepped up. These guys, I doubt they fully understood what they saw on my face that night.

They just said, 'Are you okay?'

5.

NIKKI KEATING: My family said, 'Well, why don't you go and do something else?'

Dancing around saying—you're putting yourself in this position. But I love being a bartender. I love the people I work with.

And—I'm trying to explain this to my Dad—the problem is the scariest part isn't in the bar, it's getting home at the end of the night.

It is such a mundane act—walking on the street, catching a bus. But I've been watched, followed, grabbed. I'll never understand why it happens to me so much.

And there are certain sentences you don't want to say out loud. All the times I was nearly raped.

So, you want me to quit? Where do I go? It's everywhere.

I just used anger, you know. Wore my make-up like war paint. You know when you go into a bar and the bartender is 'you are beneath me don't even look at me'—I did a lot of that.

6.

NIKKI KEATING: Fast forward four years, one night I'm sitting at knockoffs with a friend and she tells me the union has just done this survey on sexual harassment in hospitality.

Even hearing those two things in the same sentence—'sexual harassment' and 'hospitality'—it was like fireworks went off in my head.

The results were *so* dark. It was almost unbelievable. But actually, it was *real* for the first time, what was happening to me. It was happening to everyone.

I'd just worn this shit because I didn't entirely understand it. And over time that'd become—I'm wearing it because all the women around me are wearing it too.

Well that's a really dangerous place for us, if we all we do is stand together and wear it.

If we don't stand *against* it. But that's a huge thing to ask someone to do.

7.

NIKKI KEATING: Well, cue the dark shit.

Not because I wanted to be some sort of hero. The last thing I wanted was to be the face of sexual assault in hospitality…

PROJECTION: November 2017.

Media Launch: United Voice Hospo Voice Campaign— Respect Is the Rule

Nikki Keating is the face of the campaign.

A PUBLIC SPEECH

NIKKI KEATING: When I was nineteen years old, I was working in a German restaurant, serving cocktails.

One night, I felt someone's fist in my back. I was wedged against the bar by someone I couldn't see.

I was confused. I was shocked. I didn't react.

Pause.

And in the middle of the restaurant, on a busy Friday night, this man put two fingers inside me.

I didn't look at him. I turned and walked the drinks to the table.

That signal at the back of our head that says: Don't react. That's not *consent*.

Pause.

This happens every day in hospitality. I have never gone a week without experiencing some level of sexual harassment or assault. Never once.

End of public speech.

8.

NIKKI KEATING: Next day, I got trolled online—of course.

I went to work that night. It was really difficult.

We didn't know what to expect in the bar. Who would come in. What would happen.

But actually, the really big thing happened *behind* the bar.

People started standing up around me.

A guy made a comment about my colleague's breasts and she just turned and repeated it as I was pouring a beer. And we both stopped and together we said to him:

NIKKI KEATING WITH WOMAN 2: Fuck off.

NIKKI KEATING: He said—What? We said:

ENSEMBLE: FUCK OFF.

NIKKI KEATING: I don't think that I caused that. I'm not saying that at all. But I think what everyone saw was that I had spoken up, and it didn't destroy me.

> **PROJECTION: Within a year, 60 venues across Melbourne took on the rules laid down by the Respect is the Rule campaign.**
>
> **Across Australia, a growing movement of hospitality workers continues to fight to do their work free from harassment.**

9.

NIKKI KEATING: I mean, it doesn't have a happy ending. About six months later, I was sexually assaulted by a male patron near the bathrooms.

So, I still experience this, like I still experience it in every aspect of my life, it's just that at work, I didn't have to be the only one to deal with this guy, the whole bar swung into action against him.

The shit you get on the train, walking down the street, you can't always fight back.

That's why I still work in a bar. If it's gonna be my entire life then let's just do this, in here. Because otherwise, if my life was a book, it would be *The Things I Did While I Wasn't Being Assaulted*.

What an insane amount of pressure on your shoulders before you even walk out the door every day, you know?

PROJECTION: Image of young Nikki Keating; image of adult Nikki Keating.

JULIE BATES

Julie Bates performed by WOMAN 2.

1.

JULIE BATES: When the whole #MeToo thing erupted, we started asking ourselves—will we be included in this? Do we want to be?

People just say, well, what do you expect? They assume that if you're a sex worker you've given up your boundaries.

This is a big misunderstanding.

Sex work is work. It's not me throwing my legs in the air, love. It's exactly like you going to work: what you accept in your workplace as being fair and decent and right for you. This is what I negotiate in my workplace.

If we experience violence it isn't because we're sex workers, it's because we're women.

I mean this is what worries me—the young women doing social media pick-ups. The enthusiastic amateurs. They're doing pretty much what I'm doing, going to somebody's home or having them come to my place. Not having met them first.

You probably hope next morning you can boast about it to your girlfriends. That it was fun and you had a good time.

But as sex workers, we don't just go into a stranger's home and cross our fingers.

Nobody touches me without being invited. Nobody. And if they try it on they will be put in their place.

Other women could learn a lot from us. Sex workers are the queens really, of setting boundaries.

PROJECTION: Julie Bates

Born Melbourne, 1949

Lobbyist for Law Reform. Sex worker rights activist. Sex worker.

2.

JULIE BATES: I come from a family that wasn't good with boundaries.
From a very young age, there was screaming and smashing glass.
Protect yourself as best you can, keep your head down.
My mother was often covered in bruises.
You shut up.
But every now and then, she'd have enough and she'd challenge my father on something.
I'd be listening from my bedroom. I'd know what was coming.
Very sad and lonely place to inhabit. You can't make it stop, but inside, you know: this is not right. This is not right.
I remember at school going into exams and I'd get this cluster fuck of things coming at me and I just couldn't concentrate.
My grandfather taught me to draw. My uncle taught me to dance. My grandmother taught me to cook and entertain. But I grew up a pretty timid, frightened person.

3.

JULIE BATES: When I finished school, I was packed off to business college to learn typing and shorthand.
That was probably the funniest year of my life.
Suddenly, here I am meeting other young women, pooling our lunch money to buy a packet of Viscount cigarettes.
Monday lunch we'd talk about what we got up to on the weekend.
I remember one girl bringing the semen of her boyfriend in a used condom wrapped up in a handkerchief and we all had a good look. I had my first penetrative sex that year and I shared that too.
The conversations were pretty free flowing. All the stuff you weren't meant to talk about—women didn't talk about sex!
And then you find out that actually we're all interested in sex, we're all having sex.
So, that year was a great thing—a year-long course all about sex. And also a bit about economics and commercial stuff but what they were preparing you for was to be a slave to some bloke as a secretary.

4.

JULIE BATES: I got a job working for a criminal defence lawyer in St. Kilda.

Our clients were drug users, drug dealers, brothel owners, sex workers.

So. Look. I think there are very few women on the planet who haven't imagined or fantasized, 'What would it be like to be a prostitute?'—that's the word they used back then.

I had a mortgage to pay, child to raise.

So, I decided to see what might be on offer in the local massage parlour. How brave was I? I'm talking to the manager, and the bell goes. He says 'Right. Here's your first client.'

'What?! Where's the training?' He pulls out these leopard print bikini bottoms—'Wear these.'

The guy comes in and he's straight up on the massage table. I think, 'I've had a massage once. I remember that stuff,' But as I'm turning him over, he gets me in this kind of headlock, like being in the jaws of a crocodile and bang!

He comes. All through my hair!

I was shell shocked.

That was my first job.

I knew nothing about setting boundaries.

5.

JULIE BATES: I began to learn the fundamentals of my profession, on the street. I worked the corner of Darley and Liverpool Streets in Darlinghurst, Sydney. The first people who really taught me were the trans women who owned that patch.

Fuck, they were tough.

They initiated me into the time-honoured tradition of street based sex work: we debrief. On the corner between jobs, we would talk to each other about the work.

How that guy pushed you too hard.

Which clients you might want to avoid.

My friend, Joanna, didn't do oral sex. Didn't like it.

[*To* WOMAN 1] Boundaries.

[*Back to the audience*] They'd say to me—you need to know not just what do *they* want, what are *you* going to be comfortable agreeing to?

Where those two things meet, that's your contract.

Well, all sorts of workplaces have policies and guidelines. But do we actually use them—how *comfortable* do you feel to *assert* yourself?

And this is the question for all of us. All of us.

Back then the rest of the city saw us as 'fallen women', the lowest of the low.

So almost every part of sex work was a crime, and the cops were all over us, literally. We were fair game.

I worked my patch of Darlinghurst for three years. And sometimes I was okay to assert myself.

And sometimes I couldn't.

6.

JULIE BATES: The night it began to change for me, cold miserable night, I'm standing on that corner and up the street comes the Salvation Army with their thermos. And this night, the poor soul they offered the cup of tea to—was me.

And it suddenly hit me: I had become a prostitute. And I thought, there's no turning back from this now. You've done it. You can never forget it. You can never forgive yourself. You're going to live with this shame for the rest of your life.

Something *had* to shift.

'Cause if didn't, I reckon I was dead, dead in the water. I don't mean physically dead, but dead inside.

You can't live a whole life in shame. Outside yourself.

You have to be able say, this is me. And stand inside yourself.

I handed the cup back: I don't want your cold tea and sympathy, thanks.

If there is ever going to be a chance to take some pride in what I'm doing …

Didn't quite have the words for it then.

But that's what I was reaching for.

7.

JULIE BATES: One night, the women I worked with were talking about this new disease. This was not like the other STIs. This one was going to kill you.

It didn't have a name back then, but the disease was HIV/AIDS. *We* didn't have AIDS but we didn't want to get it from our clients.

But this was an era when clients demanded a condom-free service.

We started to say—we are going to use condoms. And this is the thing—we are all using them or none of us are using them. Very unusual solidarity, because so many women are taught to distrust each other.

The first time I tried to introduce a condom into a job, I could not convince the client to use it. I was shaking. This wasn't just don't touch my bum or don't put your fingers inside me.

This was literally life and death.

We are going to interrupt your sexual pleasure. To get a condom on that.

At this moment, I take priority. And I am telling you how it's going to go.

What I found out, is that I am much more assertive than I knew. MUCH more.

> **PROJECTION: Australian sex workers pioneered one of the most successful HIV prevention strategies in the world and became safe sex educators to millions of men.**
>
> **They went on to win another battle: in 1995 NSW became the first place on the planet to decriminalise sex work.**
>
> **For her leadership in this work, in 2018 Julie Bates was awarded an Order of Australia 'for distinguished service to community health'. She was the first out sex worker in Australia ever to receive this honour.**

What we have done is we've educated men to be better behaved I think. In some respects.

8.

JULIE BATES: I'm in my seventies now and there's still unfinished business to attend to. In some parts of Australia and most of the rest of the world, sex work is still [!] a crime. Those laws don't protect us, they put us in harm's way.

But when our *right* to work is respected, we can spell out our boundaries and talk to each other without fear. This is the last frontier, if you like—I will continue to fight for equal rights for sex workers for the rest of my life.

And I'm still seeing the odd client.

I know I intimidate some of my clients—being clear about exactly what I'm going to do with them, how I'm going to do it, how long I'm going to take to do it and what I'm going to charge them. There's not much room for them to move.

I don't find it difficult at all anymore, but I've had a lot of practice.

Here's the guts of it: you can't hold a boundary until you truly believe that the territory inside it is yours.

Yours.

A woman's body is always her possession. Always. Never anybody else's. I do not sell myself, I do not sell my body. I never sell any part of my body. I go home with my body, all of it, every day, every night.

Often, on the way, I'll stop and buy myself a dozen roses.

Sometimes two dozen.

PROJECTION: Image of young Julie Bates; image of adult Julie Bates.

PATRICIA MADIGAN

Patricia Madigan performed by WOMAN 3.

1.

PATRICIA MADIGAN: [*turning to* WOMAN 2] The first thing I'd like to say is that I think there are very few women on the planet who haven't imagined or fantasized: 'What would it be like to be a nun?' [*Laughs.*]

[*To audience*] I can tell you what's it like [*laughing*] and it's not what most people think. But I saw it—when I was very young.

From my first day at school, I was watching the nuns who taught me. They seemed … happy. I don't know if they always were, but they looked like they were doing interesting things with their lives.

And I guess I was also aware of married life, where women weren't always so fulfilled.

I remember the exact moment I told my mother: I'm going to be a nun. What I wanted was that life of *freedom*.

I've been a nun for more than thirty years.

I think nuns are loved—we're just people who are helping everyone, but really not to take us too seriously. And within the Church, there isn't much of an official place for female authority.

But a man who is a *priest* is seen as somebody powerful and respected. Mostly. I know some priests are now feeling very abused in public. Because of the situations we've had.

We've seen a terrible crisis of sexual abuse in the Catholic Church. Terrible.

But these two things aren't separate. And this is the root of the problem, for all of us—women in religious communities have been talking about it for a long time, long before #MeToo:

Wherever you have a serious imbalance of power … you're going to find abuse.

Personally, I haven't experienced sexual abuse. But I know something about the imbalance of power.

PROJECTION: Sr Patricia Madigan PhD

Catholic nun

Born Melbourne, 1950

2.

PATRICIA MADIGAN: I was the first person in my family to go to uni. Going to uni in the seventies, was—whoa! Protests, demonstrations, all kinds of radical new thinking … I'd just pick up books in the library that interested me. It sort of began to open up my mind. And that impulse, once it gets going, is not easily turned back off. Once you start to ask questions, anything can be questioned. Anything!

I took my first vows as a Catholic sister in 1978. I was really interested in theology—the study of the actual texts of the Bible.

Growing up, we learnt the gospel stories from the priest. But to go to the theological institute and read the scriptures myself in the original Greek, and understand the nuances—it was fascinating!

There was a bit of an issue with the story we'd been taught—women had just been written out of it!

One small taste okay—the Last Supper—Jesus, and twelve men. Once you know anything about the culture—they couldn't possibly have had thirteen men at that dinner and no women.

It was infuriating! But it was also *good* news—there must be another version of this story.

As I studied and learnt, my sense of God expanded. And really, life is a relationship with God, isn't it?

And for me, God has no gender, definitely not a *him*. I've always felt—I mean, as far back as I can remember—God is beyond anything human.

Then at the end of the course—the men went off and became priests.

And by this stage, I was thinking [*puzzled*] well why can't women be priests?

3.

PATRICIA MADIGAN: A job came up as dean of students in one of the university colleges. The first time the priests in that college would be working with a woman.

Every year the university held a church service for all the different faiths, and they heard there was a woman dean in one of the colleges—probably a bit of a novelty. So I got asked to preach.

The priests from my college didn't come. Actually, they were all silence. And from then on everything became a little bit competitive.

When it came time for the review session about my role, the priests said they didn't want to go any further with the experiment. Experiment!

4.

PATRICIA MADIGAN: But my next job—different university—was a *chaplain's* job.

Oh it was great! I loved working with the young students, supporting them, getting them thinking *outwards*. I did that job for six years, but—interesting—on my contract it said I was '*assistant to the chaplain*'. Even though in fact, I was the chaplain you know? [*Chuckles.*]

Lots of sisters would come back with the same story. They were out working with the sick, working with young children, hard-working, *gifted* women doing all the pastoral work of priests—but never given the title. Didn't get paid a lot. Couldn't get promoted.

We really loved the work and you know, we wanted to have that work, to stay in the role.

[*To* WOMAN 1] But that voice, that says stay silent, don't complain. That's not exactly consent.

5.

PATRICIA MADIGAN: I started to do interfaith work for the Catholic Church. There were women at those meetings, but the people who stood up and spoke as leaders were the men.

So, a few of us started saying, 'Let's have our own conversations.'

We formed a group. There were Aboriginal women, Buddhist and Jewish women, Hindus, Sikhs, Muslims … We even had Zoroastrians.

One day I brought up that, in my church, women are never allowed to lead the service. And the Muslim women said, 'That's the same for us—when we go to the mosque we're not allowed to speak, or sit at the front.' And the Jewish women told us, in the synagogue, the rabbi leads the service downstairs with all the men, but the women must all stay sitting upstairs. [*Laughs.*]

This started to ring some bells. 'Well what's the *reason* for that in your church?'

I told them that in the Catholic Church women couldn't represent Christ *as a man*. That's the official reason.

But Muslim women were told if a woman was at the front leading the service, the men would be distracted from their prayers. That's why women must always stay at the back. And on it went.

Well, there must be some sort of conspiracy because they were all completely different reasons, but in the end, it was the same rule—don't stand up, don't stand down the front, and whatever you do—don't speak! [*Laughs.*]

6.

PATRICIA MADIGAN: When I was young, there was talk about women priests in the Catholic Church.

Then within a generation, the direction changed—now it was forbidden to even discuss it.

Most of my friends wouldn't go much to church anymore. They'd ask me:

WOMAN 1: [*to the audience as much as to Patricia Madigan*] Why do you stay? Why don't you and go do something else?

PATRICIA MADIGAN: Well I can still read what I want to read and there will be times when you get a chance to voice something, so I'm going to take those moments. I don't want to make more trouble for myself than I'm already in, but nobody's going to shoot me for it.

And ultimately—Why should I leave? It's my church.

ENSEMBLE: Amen.

7.

PATRICIA MADIGAN: One day in a meeting, I was saying, 'This is what I'd like to happen.' And one of the senior priests suddenly turned to me, 'Look', he said, 'The Church is not a democracy!'

And I said to him, 'No. But it's not a monarchy, or an oligarchy, or a dictatorship—*or is it?*' I thought that was quite good. Well, he just could not quite answer. And off he went.

But a few days later, someone came to me and said, 'I have to issue you with an official caution.'

This person—me!—needed to be cautioned, upbraided.

He said, 'Be careful when you talk to someone who *might get upset.*'

Long pause.

What I am going to do now, is preach to you.
Yes. [*Beautiful pause.*]

8.

PATRICIA MADIGAN: One of the most beautiful parts of the Bible is where Jesus says: 'Let the little children come to me.'

Do you hear it? Not little *boys*. Little *children*.

When I was a little child, in my family, my father went out to work and my mother was at home.

But when I was five, I entered this other universe, ruled entirely by women: school.

My school was run by nuns. The first assembly, it was so noisy! But when the principal stood up and came to the microphone, the whole school went silent to hear her speak.

I kind of thought, wow.

When I was eight, my mother was giving me a bath, and I looked up and told her: I'm going to be a nun.

[*Taking hold of the entire audience*] What God is calling us to, is fullness of life. Sometimes what we have to do is make decisions so that our lives and the lives of other people around us can be as full as possible.

9.

PATRICIA MADIGAN: I did not stop doing my work in the Church. I did not stop saying things in my work that might make some people upset. I expanded my work.

I went to Europe and America and the Middle East—to study. I did my PhD in theology—my subject was women's wisdom across the faiths.

And I've been very busy ever since.

I'm just about to go and work with some nuns in Papua New Guinea—women don't have much opportunity to study theology there. And after that I'm going to speak at a conference in Germany, about the ordination of women in the Orthodox Churches.

You know, I might get a bit of pushback, some people from Eastern Europe might be horrified. So that'll be interesting!

I see this in the Catholic girls' school down the road. The girls leave that school believing their role today is to give their gifts to the world and out they go, into all the different occupations.

Beautiful.

But.

At the risk of upsetting anyone, I have to ask:

How free are those girls going to be, to actually do what God has made them so able to do?

When is one of those girls going to walk back into the school as a priest?

PROJECTION: Image of young Patricia Madigan; image of adult Patricia Madigan.

PAM BURRIDGE

Pam Burridge performed by WOMAN 4.

1.

WOMAN 6, WOMAN 7 *and* WOMAN 8 *rise and address the audience.*

WOMAN 6: What if you *know* what you want to be …

WOMAN 7: But you're not sure you're good enough?

WOMAN 8: What if you're *sure* you're not good enough?

WOMAN 6: Are you wrong to imagine you're not good enough?

WOMAN 7: [*touch of suspense*] Or …

WOMAN 8: Are you seeing something *real*, about how things run, in the world that you're in?

 Pause.

WOMAN 6, 7 & 8: [*looking to each other, smiling*] Yes.

 They sit.

PAM BURRIDGE: When I was little, basically, I wanted to be a boy.

 Look, I didn't actually want to be a boy. But all the fun stuff was for boys.

The first thing I ever wanted to be was halfback for the Manly Sea Eagles, because they were the ones with blond hair like me.

At that age, we have these dreams and this flow, this feeling of movement and all the stuff we're going to do. Imagine if you could fly. Imagine if you could play for Manly.

Then I started school.

Quickly worked it out—girls can't play football, apparently. I'm never going to play for Manly.

But not too long after that, I discovered surfing, so hello, individual sport, don't need to be picked to play. You don't need anything. You just need a surfboard and some waves and your mum to drive you to the beach. But apart from that ...

PROJECTION: Pam Burridge

Born 1965, Northern Beaches, Sydney

Champion Surfer

2.

PAM BURRIDGE: In the sixties, when I was born, so many Australian girls and women surfed, like the ancient traditions from Hawaii— Queens surfing—all those Gidgets on their long boards—nine-foot long.

On those boards, everyone could get on the same wave together— boys and girls, surfing parallel, side by side, straight ahead.

Then in the seventies, they began to chop the long boards down … like a foot every two months.

Short boards go across the wave, you take the whole wave for yourself. That's really different. It's only one surfer on the wave.

So sitting out the back waiting for the wave, the culture changed, the order was set.

I get these older women in my classes who surfed as teenagers, until all of a sudden the guys started going out of their way to surf over the top of them, make sure they didn't come out again—really heavy stuff.

And very quickly, women's surfing just sort of vanished in Australia.

By the time I started going to the beach, you didn't really see women out on the waves, they were all on the sand. The towel holders, Chiko Roll minders, that was the girls' job.

I sort of skirted under that.

3.

PAM BURRIDGE: For my tenth birthday, I talked my parents into getting me a surfboard. Single fin, square tail, backyard special. It was orange and purple, with a yellow nose.

I remember taking it down to the beach for the first time, no idea how to pick a wave. I just remember turning around and catching something.

And I remember standing up.

Yeah … wilderness and … yeah.

It was just a calling for me, you know?

I was always an anxious child. But the sea kind of salved me.

And nobody kicked me off the water for being a girl, because for two years …

Small pause.

… almost nobody realised I was a girl.

I just got around like a dead set boy—board shorts, little wetsuit, blond mop. Never spoke.

Sometimes the boys would talk about girls. Like some secret society. I tried not to listen—not about me, didn't apply to me.

The first time I tried to enter a contest, Mum had to explain my gender. So now it was out.

They threw me in the women's comp. I was twelve.

It was a little bit serious and pretty exciting.

I didn't know the rules. I figured I would just catch lots of waves and ride them really far.

Well, I won. I was shocked! And—absolutely convinced that one day, I'd be the world champion.

Two years later, age fourteen, I won the Australian title.

Next thing, I got invited to the World Cup.

In Hawaii.

4.

PAM BURRIDGE: At that age … the first time you go to Hawaii …

Some surf is deceptive, it doesn't look that big until you're out in the water and you see … waves standing up abruptly, all the way out in the ocean, 'cause they're breaking on reef. Big. Bigger than anything I'd seen in my life. Fast, 'cause they're running from deep water.

Oh wow, you know, freaking out. But you're out there.

I've got to get one.

Or, maybe I should just go back in.

No, I've got to get one.

Oh my God, I just want to go back in.

You find out which part of you is bigger—the part that does not want to be there? Or the part that does? Because to get anywhere close to a wave, to *catch* it, you have to put yourself in harm's way.

And then …

PROJECTION: Image of an immense wave rising from Pam's feet.

You just—you're in it.

PROJECTION: 1980

1980!

I quit school and join the tour. I'm the first Australian woman to go full time pro surfer. We're all going to be so big. Big stars! It's going to be massive. I'm sixteen.

Now things start to speed up.

PROJECTION [*comes on line by line to form a list*]:

Pam Burridge, world ranking:

1980–11th

1981–5th

1982–2nd

I'm a flow kind of surfer. When I'm feeling good I have this supreme confidence. No Australian woman has won the pro world title. Not yet.

5.

PROJECTION: 1983

PAM BURRIDGE: 1983 is going to be my year.

1983—the women's tour expands, the number of events almost doubles.

But—hang on, am I going mad? The prize money for each event actually goes down.

While the guys are surfing for? Ten times our prize money.

At competitions, there are two events for the guys—the Trials and the Opens, and two for us—the Women's and the Bikini Contest.

The Bikini Contest—I just didn't get it.

But those were the only women who made the papers or the TV news. The coverage of actual *surfing*—that was all about the guys.

The men got programmed when the best waves were on—so of course they had the big performances.

Their rationalisation was all about the numbers and who was watching. Some stuff about protecting us …

But that's not what it felt like. It felt like control, just wanting control. Of all of it.

I mean who owns the water, you know? Who owns the ocean?

It just made us all closer, all the girls would go above and beyond to try to promote the sport.

But we were also competing against each other, on the waves, and for sponsors …

Anyway.

6.

PAM BURRIDGE: I was in line for a sponsorship from a company and I got a call back and so—

I went to the appointment. Alone. Glass tower Sydney CBD.

I was seventeen. Really I should have been at school.

Went in there for the interview with this older businessman and it got to the point where he said, 'So, if I was in Honolulu and you were in Honolulu, it would be nice to … Can I fuck you?'

Not in so many words, but pretty straightforward.

I was like—'No.'

[*Inner voice*] I'm okay. I'm okay.

I just walked out.

Full of shame, like I'd brought it on myself. But angry inside.

I went into the first pub and got blind drunk, leglessly drunk. My parents didn't know where I was.

Yeah.

I spent a lot of my late teens and early twenties drinking, partying.

I had always been an anxious child—ambitious, but anxious—and the water had been my sanctuary.

But that was the world I was in now. That's how things ran.

Pause.

7.

PAM BURRIDGE: I didn't cope with the pressure. Or maybe I did.

> PROJECTION [*These lines are added one by one, each staying on so they build into a list. As the name of each champion appears in projection Pam Burridge speaks the name*]:
>
> **1983 World Surfing Champion—Kim Mearig (USA)**

Kim Mearig—fastest improvement in a year in the history of women's surfing.

> **PROJECTION: (Pam Burridge 3rd)**
>
> **PROJECTION: 1984 World Surfing Champion—Frieda Zamba (USA)**

Frieda Zamba—physical specimen.

> **PROJECTION: (Pam Burridge 3rd)**
>
> **PROJECTION: 1985 World Surfing Champion—Frieda Zamba (USA)**

And hungry.

> **PROJECTION: (Pam Burridge 3rd)**
>
> **PROJECTION: 1986 World Surfing Champion—Frieda Zamba (USA)**

Very hungry, Frieda Zamba.

PROJECTION: (Pam Burridge 2nd)

PROJECTION: 1987 World Surfing Champion—Wendy Botha (South Africa)

Wendy Botha—determined.

PROJECTION: (Pam Burridge 7th)

By now the list reads:

1983 World Surfing Champion—Kim Mearig (USA)

(Pam Burridge 3rd)

1984 World Surfing Champion—Frieda Zamba (USA)

(Pam Burridge 3rd)

1985 World Surfing Champion—Frieda Zamba (USA)

(Pam Burridge 3rd)

1986 World Surfing Champion—Frieda Zamba (USA)

(Pam Burridge 2nd)

1987 World Surfing Champion—Wendy Botha (South Africa)

(Pam Burridge 7th)

PROJECTION [*Now the lines of champions' names fade out, leaving only the entries for Pam Burridge*]:

(Pam Burridge 3rd)

(Pam Burridge 3rd)

(Pam Burridge 3rd)

(Pam Burridge 2nd)

(Pam Burridge 7th)

I'm a flow kind of surfer. When the doubt creeps in, the rhythm's broken, the flow's broken. Just literally a feeling I'm getting from my board.

It definitely had a breaking point
I don't know … a lot of … confusion
Like this committee inside my head—

WOMAN 6, WOMAN 7 *and* WOMAN 8 *stand.*

Each question coming quickly, one after another.

WOMAN 8: —Why am I doing this?—

WOMAN 6: —Am I meant to be doing this?—

WOMAN 7: —Am I shit?—

WOMAN 8: —Why would I think I'm shit?—

WOMAN 6: —God I must be shit!—

Faster, louder.

WOMAN 8: —Why am I doing this?—

WOMAN 6: —Am I meant to be doing this?—

WOMAN 7: —Am I shit?—

WOMAN 8: —Why would I think I'm shit?—

WOMAN 6: —God I must be shit!—

PAM BURRIDGE: SHUT UP!!

PAM BURRIDGE *turns her back to them.*

Sharp pause.

Lower voices. Intense.

WOMAN 8: —Why am I doing this?—

WOMAN 6: —Am I meant to be doing this?—

WOMAN 7: —Am I shit?—

PAM BURRIDGE: [*to audience, trying to stay calm*] I'd think—I'll be able to push myself to the next level once I've got rid of all the self-doubt—

WOMAN 8: —Why would I think I'm shit?—

WOMAN 6: —God I must be shit!—

PAM BURRIDGE: —But that's rubbish! It's never going!

Faster, louder, more intense.

WOMAN 8: —Why am I doing this?—

WOMAN 6: —Am I meant to be doing this?—

WOMAN 7: —Am I shit?—

WOMAN 8: —Why would I think I'm shit?—

PAM BURRIDGE: —Really painful.—

WOMAN 6: —God I must be shit!—

PAM BURRIDGE: —But it had a point! I didn't want to be superficial. [*Turning back to them*] I didn't want to just carry on.

They speak directly to PAM BURRIDGE—*loud and clear.*

WOMAN 8: Why am I doing this?

WOMAN 6: Am I meant to be doing this?

WOMAN 7: Am I shit?

WOMAN 8: Why would I think I'm shit?

WOMAN 6: God I must be shit!

WOMAN 8: Why—

PAM BURRIDGE: [*interrupting*] THANK YOU.

> *Now the committee stays silent. They watch* PAM BURRIDGE, *waiting.*

[*Really asking herself the question*] Why am I doing this?

WOMAN 6, 7 & 8: [*to each other, satisfied*] Yes.

> WOMAN 6, WOMAN 7 *and* WOMAN 8 *sit.*

8.

PAM BURRIDGE: I got sober when I was twenty-two.

I fell back in love with just surfing my brains out—by myself.

The next year a contest at Bondi tried out something new in Australia, just for once: equal prize money for men and women.

The guys were livid! So I held a press conference.

I know many people will be surprised to discover we don't get anything like the prize money of the men. So this is big news for us. If you feel you belong, you respond.

I know. So hardcore.

That year I met my husband Mark.

Together, we took my surfing technique apart. Interesting—I was only using part of the wave—aggressively surfing up, but letting the wave just push me back down.

I had to completely relearn how I thought about a wave—to *attack* going down.

So I could finally work out which part was bigger—the part of me that didn't want to be there, or the part that did.

9.

PROJECTION: 1990

PAM BURRIDGE: 1990 … [*Smiles.*]

When I was twelve, I was convinced I was going to be the World Champion.

I was right.

That year, the World Championship came down to the last event of the tour—in Hawaii.

With fifteen seconds to go, I caught the wave that won the title.

PROJECTION: 1990 World Surfing Champion—Pam Burridge (Aus)

Her winning margin (1914 points) was the biggest that had ever been recorded in the history of women's surfing.

Winning was ecstasy, tempered by extraordinary relief, thank Christ that's over, I did it.

And then you're like—what was that all about? What was that for?

PROJECTION: Australian Women's World Surfing champions since Pam Burridge 1990:

They dissolve on line by line to form a long list.

Wendy Botha 1991, 1992

Pauline Menczer 1993

Lane Beachley 1998, 1999, 2000, 2001, 2002, 2003

Chelsea Georgeson 2005

Layne Beachley 2006

Stephanie Gilmore 2007, 2008, 2009, 2010, 2012, 2014

Tyler Wright 2016, 2017

Stephanie Gilmore 2018

PROJECTION: 2018

World Surf League announces equal prize money for men and women.

Finally, second line fades out leaving only the year
PROJECTION: 2018

10.

PAM BURRIDGE: 2018. One last bit of history that year. I found myself watching the first game of professional women's rugby league football … You ripper … [*Smiles.*]

There was this moment … when the blonde halfback caught the ball.

Gasps.

[*Whispered, hardly breathing*] I was so happy! And then, out of nowhere—

—all these tears.

Pause.

It's interesting now to see these older women who turn up in my classes, they've spent their lives watching everyone else surf.

Sometimes I come down to the beach, and there are more women surfing than men.

The other day a woman was out there, with her two daughters and her son.

They were doing pretty well.

But she—

—she was *gunning* it.

It was pretty cool.

PROJECTION: Image of young Pam Burridge; image of adult Pam Burridge.

JULIA GILLARD

Julia Gillard performed by WOMAN 5.

1.

JULIA GILLARD: [*smiling*] We want to tell our daughters they can be *anything*. But for Australian women, every time we have that conversation, there's a bloody big elephant in the room …

[*Playfully*] Let me see if I can conjure the elephant …

[*Suddenly hard and loud*] I will not be lectured about sexism and misogyny by this man!

I will not!

Not now, not ever!

PROJECTION: Julia Gillard

Born Barry, Wales, 1961

First female prime minister of Australia

[*Wryly*] Everywhere I go, this is the thing I get asked about—That Speech, and How I Got To That Point?

Smiles.

Everyone knows how I got there—

PROJECTION: Ditch the Witch

Bob Brown's Bitch

Deliberately Barren

Non-productive old-cow

You've got a big arse, Julia.

There she is! The big-arsed elephant—'This is what we all know happened to our first and only female prime minister!'

Pause.

Yes. I do marvel at it. No, maybe not 'marvel'. 'Puzzle' is the right word. I puzzle at it.

The story of my prime ministership has ended up being the story of the abuse I received.

And oh, that is a big story, and we do need to talk about it.

But there's a bigger story in my prime ministership, which not many people seem to be telling their daughters. I'm going to tell it to you.

2.

JULIA GILLARD: I used to love going to schools, six-year-old kids would confidently say to you 'I'm going to be prime minister when I grow up!'

I was never that kid.

Then at high school … I got into debating…

I'm the sort of person who likes to have a feisty go. I don't mind having an argument.

And slowly the penny dropped and I thought well actually I could be a parliamentarian and it didn't occur to me that there was any reason I couldn't, just because I was a girl.

When I was at university, intellectually I understood the barriers for women, but personally, I didn't actually feel many of them.

As a young lawyer, it was a fairly knockabout, larrikin kind of culture. But I felt quite at home with that.

Even when I was first elected to the Parliament, I wouldn't have said gender was a huge issue for me. I didn't go into politics to make it kinder or gentler. I wanted to show that a woman could command that bear pit, she could thrive.

In the theatre of Question Time, I gave as good as I got. There's a physicality to projecting yourself in that environment—your adrenaline kicks in and your senses are heightened. I enjoyed it, and at my best I dominated.

I knew the women who came before us had had it very tough. But I thought we were the generation that everything was going to be different for. I thought, 'we've got this sussed'.

Chuckles.

Dear oh dear—I could only really see it clearly, when I got to the top.

PROJECTION: **24 June 2010**

Almost 110 years since Federation

and after 26 consecutive male prime ministers,

Julia Gillard becomes Australia's first female PM.

My memories of that day are in fragments …Moments of elation … an occasional sense of unreality …a hunger for what was to come …

PROJECTION [*Headlines*]: **'RED Hot!'**

'Realisation of the Great Feminist Dream'

'Is This How You Smash a Glass Ceiling?'

'It's a GIRL!'

3.

JULIA GILLARD: I knew there'd be a lot of attention around it—first female PM. But I thought then it would wash its way through the system and it would be back to business as usual. [*Small chuckle.*]

The day after I became prime minister, I visited a shopping centre and the media coverage—TV, front page of the newspapers—was dominated by the jacket I was wearing. And what people *thought* of the jacket. I mean completely dominated.

[*Laughing*] These gendered references were going to just swirl around for a while and then peter out. How long can the country talk about someone's jacket?! [*Laughing.*]

There was a lot I'd come into politics to do. My government got stuck into governing.

But in the hard political contests—the election, the carbon tax— the insults that started to get thrown around were things I hadn't heard before, stuff that could only be directed at a woman.

> PROJECTION: **'Anyone who chooses a life without children, as Gillard has, cannot have much love in them,' Mark Latham 2011**

The longer I served as prime minister, the more shrill it became …

> PROJECTION: **'Small breasts, huge thighs and a big red box'—Liberal National Party Fundraiser**

Even that wasn't the worst of it …

Pornographic cartoons of me sent daily to the entire Parliament and Press Gallery …

Threats of violent abuse, of rape. Almost daily.

Pause.

A horror show—nobody could rip their eyes from it.

4.

JULIA GILLARD: What everybody saw was the abuse, but what was harder to see was— [*To* WOMAN 1] it didn't destroy me.

[*Back to audience*] I mean, there were moments when I felt the weight of it ... Everyone likes to be liked, and I'm no different...

But I toughed it out, I congratulated myself on how well I was coping.

But my mistake was about timing. It was feeding my opponents ... and because I hadn't said anything about it all this time, the longer it went on, the harder it got to call it out.

There are many ways to understand what happened next. Here are two.

Number One: If a woman bites her tongue for too long, some time, somewhere, those emotions will just burst through.

Number Two: Over many years, I'd honed the skills of dominating Parliament when I needed to.

5.

JULIA GILLARD: On 9 October 2012, the leader of the Opposition, Tony Abbott moved a motion in the Parliament telling my government we needed to take the denigration of women more seriously.

For fuck's sake! Once I started, it just got a life of its own.

'I will not be lectured about sexism and misogyny by this man.'

ENSEMBLE: 'I will not.'

WOMAN 1: 'Not now!'

WOMAN 7: 'Not ever!'

JULIA GILLARD *watches as the* ENSEMBLE *thunder out her words.*

WOMAN 2: 'Repulsive double standards!'

WOMAN 6: 'Misogyny!'

WOMAN 4: 'Sexism!'

JULIA GILLARD: I meant every word of it.

WOMAN 8: 'Now he is looking at his watch ...'

WOMAN 3: 'because apparently, a woman's spoken too long.'

JULIA GILLARD: I didn't feel heated or angry. I felt powerful.

By the time I got back to the office—

PROJECTION [*Headlines*]: **'Australian Politician Shrinks in Embarrassment, as Prime Minister Destroys Him for Being a Misogynist'**

'Best Thing You'll See All Day: Australia's Female Prime Minister Rips Misogynist a New One'

'Australia's Prime Minister Julia Gillard is One Badass Motherfucker'

Today, there are operas based on That Speech, also TikTok challenges, an interpretative modern ballet, and tea towels. All over the world, when I'm asked to tell the story of my prime ministership, *this* is the story I am asked to tell most often.

And somehow the story of That Speech—three years of ridiculous attacks, fifteen minutes of blazing counter attack—becomes The Story of Australia's First Woman Prime Minister …

6.

JULIA GILLARD: But here's the thing … what about my prime ministership? My actual prime ministership.

For three years and two days I was the leader of my country. When we were faced with a hung parliament, I found a way to negotiate a working majority and hold it together, and my government achieved a lot. The country's first National Disability Insurance Scheme, paid parental leave, a Royal Commission into Institutional Responses to Child Sexual Abuse, a price on carbon, once in a generation school reforms …

Just to name a few. Because we did a lot more. A lot.

PROJECTION: **The government with the highest rate in Australian history for getting its legislation passed—**

PROJECTION: **Julia Gillard's.**

Yes. I puzzle at it still.

Of all the stories about Australia's first female prime minister, the one that barely gets told is that one.

The story that actually answers all the sexist abuse.

The story that you might say, *explains* all the sexist abuse: I got a lot done.

You may not agree with everything I did. Or didn't do.

But those are the things I went into politics to do. And I did them.

That's the story I want you to tell your daughters—our first woman prime minister got a lot done.

Now *that's* badass.

7.

JULIA GILLARD: Once I left politics, I thought a lot about how little hard data there is on women as leaders. Not just the *barriers* in our way, but how *effective* women are when we actually get the opportunity to lead.

I'm working with women all over the world now to build a picture of what women's leadership actually looks like—how women leaders bring people along with us, the things we pay attention to, the things we can change.

[*To* WOMAN 4] The problem, if you can call it that, has never been that we're not good enough.

[*Back to audience*] For me, this has to be more than an intellectual journey now. Thinking alone is not going to be enough for me. I want to feel it

Because when I go to schools, as I still do, six-year-old girls still bowl up to me and say 'When I grow up, I'm going to be the prime minister!'

And we all want to tell them—yes you can!

Pause. She looks across the faces of the audience.

Listen, [*to* WOMAN 4] feminism has always come in waves.

[*Back to audience*] You can feel another wave gathering now, fed by the anger we all share that we still aren't in that equal world we thought we would be. The *anger* gives me profound hope.

But every wave creates a backlash.

Those little girls are going to cop that backlash.

WOMAN 4: I had to completely relearn how I thought about a wave— learning to surf not just up, but down.

JULIA GILLARD: We've got to get the fortitude, now, to see it clearly for what it really is and push it back. All of us.

WOMAN 4: To *attack* going down.
JULIA GILLARD: Early.
      And *hard*.
      Don't take a backward step.
      Step up. Have a red hot go. RED HOT.

      PROJECTION: Image of young Julia Gillard; image of the mature Julia Gillard, standing in a sea of schoolgirls.

INTERVAL

ACT TWO: THROWING THE ELEPHANT

*MARCIA LANGTON**

Marcia Langton performed by WOMAN 6.

Lights up—eight women seated. The women look out into the audience and then all slowly turn to look to each other, except WOMAN 6 *(*MARCIA LANGTON*) who ignores them.*

The other women begin to notice.

1.

WOMAN 3: [*to* WOMAN 6, *inviting her to share*] So … do you remember the first time you heard about #MeToo?
MARCIA LANGTON: No.

    Silence.

WOMAN 3: The first story you—
MARCIA LANGTON: No I don't.

    Silence.

I know a black woman started it, then something about Hollywood, right?
    I cannot be bothered participating frankly, I'm just not interested.

    Uncomfortable silence.

[*With feeling*] Because—what is happening to Indigenous women?
    I don't want to listen to a bunch of feminists, when they have nothing whatsoever to say about that.

    Awkward silence, briefer.

[*Changing tack*] I mean I feel like I live in war zone.
    I stand in my house and point my finger that way, that is where Jill Meagher was murdered. If you go to my gate and look right,

---

* Performance note: 'This piece needs to be delivered calmly. You may feel choked or angry as you read it, but if there is anger, the anger has to be a controlled anger. Talk to the audience like they're intelligent. Bring them with you.' *Marcia Langton*

Courtney Herron was murdered there. Euridice Dixon—murdered on the street where my office is.

WOMAN 1: [*joining in*] Where I catch the bus home every night.

MARCIA LANGTON: And that's just the *public* violence against women— the horror stories that make the news. Strangers in the dark. But actually most of the horror—

WOMAN 2: —happens in our homes.

WOMAN 4: Not homicidal strangers—

WOMAN 8: —homicidal husbands and boyfriends.

> **PROJECTION: One in six Australian women has experienced physical or sexual violence by a current or former intimate partner.**
>
> **On average, one Australian woman a week is murdered by her current or former partner.**

MARCIA LANGTON: Violence against women has accelerated to the point where statistically, on a theory of probabilities—no woman is safe.

No woman is safe.

> *A quick burst of strong agreement from the other women.* MARCIA LANGTON *watches them.*

WOMAN 7: I know.

WOMAN 3: I agree.

WOMAN 4: Me too.

> *Pause.*

MARCIA LANGTON: Okay, some more facts. Listen to this:

Indigenous women are eleven times more likely to die due to assault than other Australian women.

I'll say that again—Indigenous women are eleven times more likely to die due to assault than other Australian women.

Indigenous women are thirty times more likely to be hospitalized due to family violence.

In the Northern Territory, it's been estimated that Indigenous women are eighty times more likely to be hospitalised as a result of assault.

Sorry—you asked me a question. This is part of my answer.

PROJECTION: **Professor Marcia Langton**
     Born 1951, Brisbane
     Yiman woman
     Foundation Chair of Australian Indigenous Studies, University of Melbourne

2.

MARCIA LANGTON: I'm an anthropologist.
     I'm interested in facts.
     From very early on, I had this sense that the world needed to be decoded.
     I grew up in South Western Queensland, we moved around between all sorts of situations, including a native camp. That was my world.
     My grandmother and my mother both worked in the houses of rich people. *Hard* work. Cooking, cleaning. They were strong.
     My grandmother would tell yarns about life in the bush.
     One day, down at the creek, she found a man who'd hanged himself.
     She said, 'Poor bugger, we couldn't figure out why he'd done something like that.'
     Pause.
     I taught myself to read before I went to school. Wherever we were, I was emptying the library.

3.

MARCIA LANGTON: I was only the third Aboriginal person in Queensland to go to university. It felt like the world was changing. I studied anthropology, because I wanted to work on the land claims.
     The work took me all over the country—Arnhem Land, Cape York, the Gulf of Carpentaria, the Kimberley, Central Australia.
     As you drove into some places you could hear ceremonial singing.
     Sometimes I was invited to come to the ceremony.

You never learn much in one sitting, you know? People don't explicitly teach, except if you do something wrong they say, 'don't do that', but mainly the way you learn is to sit silently in a group of women and listen.

It changed me. There's a lot to know about women's law.

Then I'd get back into town, and I started noticing things—a row of women sitting together. A streak of ochre behind their ears and I'd think—I was just at a ceremony with those women.

So, I'd go and sit with them and they'd start telling me things. Things they don't easily tell people.

4.

MARCIA LANGTON: Look, to be clear, I grew up in a violent situation. I've had violent, abusive partners. I know what that is.

But I had never seen anything like the scale of the violence I began to see in the Northern Territory.

Freedom to drink alcohol was a very recent thing in the Northern Territory, right?

But now it was legal, it was an unmitigated disaster.

I was seeing this everywhere—women bandaged and bleeding. Women fleeing their homes. I was a junior anthropologist working for an Aboriginal organization on land rights claims and I'd get phone calls in the middle of the night, asking me to help.

Because nothing at all seemed to be done about it. It was accepted.

It's very hard to explain to people who haven't lived through it.

5.

MARCIA LANGTON: What Aboriginal women have been trying to do since the Stolen Generations is keep their families together.

If they call the police, they'll probably remove the children.

If the man goes to jail, his family blames her for putting another Aboriginal man in prison.

You have male leaders in the communities, enforcing silence.

And the victim ends up murdered or in hospital or in prison. Yes. The victim ends up in prison.

So women become kind of mute victims.

And over time, it becomes so normalized that people are no longer shocked by the most shocking violence. Right?

6.

MARCIA LANGTON: Most white Australians understand nothing of that complexity.

On the nightly news, the suffering of Aboriginal women and children just plays out as a kind of pornography.

Pause.

7.

MARCIA LANGTON: In my workplace it wasn't accepted that I should speak publicly about these matters.

Most anthropologists turned a blind eye to it all, for fear they'd get in trouble with the big men and wouldn't be able to do field work out in the communities.

You'd be very unpopular.

Pause.

There's a saying I learnt in my twenties: 'The world is run by those who show up.'

I've been around a long time, I show up, I pay attention to my duties.

Not just as an anthropologist. There is something fundamental about the security of your own body that comes first.

Now you can call that a feminist position or you can call it, you know, a humanist position.

Well that is my position.

Stands.

8.

A public speech.

MARCIA LANGTON: It is critical that strong women and men stand up and tell the truth.

In parts of remote Australia we are confronting rates of rape and violence against women and children that seem beyond explanation.

Instead of jail sentences … murderers and rapists are being … released back into the communities where their crimes were committed …

… many crimes go unreported, the victims too afraid to speak out.

Some of the campaigners against Indigenous incarceration use the word 'genocide'. But the question most Australians will not ask is: is our legal system … tolerating, even encouraging the femicide of Aboriginal women?

I think it is.

End of public speech.

9.

MARCIA LANGTON: In the press, and in some of the universities, I was called a crazy radical, because I said things that were plainly the case.

I was attacked for betraying Aboriginal culture: this violence was 'cultural', this was Aboriginal 'law'.

Traditional Aboriginal culture does not authorize the brutalization of women and children.

I was told that Aboriginal men are the victims of 'colonisation' and 'need to heal' before we deal with their violence.

[*Quiet, serious*] Okay look, the rage of colonised people is very real. These men *have* been colonised. These men *are* traumatised.

But what? Until you overcome your trauma, it's okay to bash women and children, it's okay to kill women and children?

I was accused by some Aboriginal men of labelling all Aboriginal men as rapists. Of course, I'm not talking about *all* Aboriginal men. I wouldn't be able to *talk* if I was talking about all Aboriginal men.

But oh, it's only *some* men—it's just a few of us. So a few women die? …

Well in fact, the femicide rate in the Aboriginal community is through the roof.

I feel sick, I feel physically sick.

It's another way of saying that the lives of women and children are worth nothing.

That's what *all* those excuses add up to—

The lives of women and children are worth nothing.

Pause.

10.

MARCIA LANGTON: I asked quite a few feminists—why have you got nothing to say about the situation of Aboriginal women? Aren't we women, too?

And they'd have no answer just 'Oh … That's an Aboriginal problem … I respect your people's right to self-determination.'

I tried to find a white-feminist defence of Aboriginal women with any of the common sense and cut through of Rosie Batty.

Rosie Batty understands—she goes out into communities, working with Aboriginal women, listening to them.

Where are the rest of them?

Where are the rest of you?

Long pause.

11.

MARCIA LANGTON: But I began to get emails, phone calls—from Aboriginal women.

We all have an inbuilt survival reflex, you know. But some survivors of extreme violence have lost those inhibitions. They say—why should I shut up? How much worse can it be?

For years, Indigenous women leaders have been pushed into the background.

This is starting to change.

There is a growing network of women tackling this violence. Really smart women, powerful Aboriginal women who run organizations. Who aren't afraid. We talk, we support each other, we share information.

We've finally got the Australian government to agree to a dedicated Aboriginal and Torres Strait Islander action plan on domestic and family violence, so *we* can be the ones to address the issues that we're facing.

12.

WOMAN 3: What do non-Aboriginal women need to do?

WOMAN 8: Why do white women always want black women to come up with solutions for them?!

WOMAN 3: Okay you want me to listen. You want me to understand. Then let me ask, [*to* MARCIA LANGTON] because actually I don't know what to do.

MARCIA LANGTON: Include Aboriginal women.

Invite black women to your meetings. Hold your meetings in black territory. On Aboriginal land or in an Aboriginal woman's office.

Other women can learn a lot from Aboriginal women.

Listen to Aboriginal women about what they need and take it seriously.

Pay some attention to the facts.

Ask yourselves, what you *really* believe:

Is this just the way things are? Do we *accept* it?

Pause.

Well who is going to change it?

History is made by those who show up.

Show up.

PROJECTION: Image of young Marcia Langton; image of adult Marcia Langton

Projection dissolves.

Long stillness.

Sounds of the bush—at least ninety seconds of stillness and bush sounds.

MARION BLACKWELL

Marion Blackwell performed by WOMAN 7.

1.

Beginning quietly, with a careful sense of WOMAN 6, *but without looking directly at her.* WOMAN 6 *remains quiet and in her own space.*

MARION BLACKWELL: When I was little … I don't remember thinking about what I wanted to be. I just kept on being. I wanted to break in horses and do things. I wanted to be on the land.

I grew up near the NSW–Queensland border, high up in the Great Dividing Ranges.

[*Beginning to warm up*] I loved getting up and just going out into the bush. You'd fill your back-sack with oranges and out you'd go.

Formidable country. Very rugged. Beautiful great big trees hanging off the sides of these steep rocky hills. So it was all scrambling and climbing, and finding a way around.

It was *isolated*: school came to me by postal correspondence, and later, School of the Air. We had a crackly old wireless you could hardly hear with all the interference from the mountains. So that was sort of a bit hit and miss to it.

But my father taught me astronomy and surveying.

And we had an Aboriginal stockman, Old Yim, and he taught me all sorts of things. He was fantastic. He knew medicinal plants and food plants, and he taught me how to find the bees' hives.

You go down to the creek where the bees are sucking the water from the mud and you float a bit of a down-feather behind the wing. And then you watch it up-light and it's pointing the direction … marvellous. Follow it to the hive and you take a *little bit*. You don't take all their honey, just a little bit for breakfast to come.

For my seventh birthday, my grandmother gave me a honey pot, with rings on it, and a bee sitting on the lid.

One morning when the men came down for smoko, there was a shearer from Western Australia—great big Aboriginal man, and he picked up my beloved honey pot, and he said:

'Little girl, in Western Australia there are mountains just like your honey pot—all striped red and very beautiful.'

Well, children have these visions. That was now an aim of my life, to go and find these honey pot mountains.

PROJECTION: **Marion Blackwell**

Born 1928, Northern NSW

Mycologist, Ecologist

2.

MARION BLACKWELL: I loved growing things.

Pandorea pandorana. We used to call them Monkey Bells, these creepers with beautiful cream bells and inside—brown and furry like a monkey.

When I was five I started looking for the seed pods, out in the bush, and growing them.

My Uncle Griff came up to see Dad and brought his friend with him, Guy Yates. Yates—from the seed company. Bright cookie—he fell upon my creeping flowers, and took some seeds off with him.

They're grown all over the world now, and they all came off our verandah.

When I was seven I started fostering orphan wallabies. In those days, they used to say you couldn't foster the joeys because the cow's milk was too rich for them.

But I worked out a way, you put red hot charcoal in the milk to take the fat off.

An old chap called Mr. Moody from the Agriculture Department said it was the first time he'd seen anyone keep these joeys alive. He wrote up my formulas in the Agricultural Gazette.

So. I did not spend my childhood stuck inside with dolls.

That was my whole horizon. It was fully engrossing.

3.

MARION BLACKWELL: I did well in the school leaving and after that, I thought for living on the land Vet Science would be a very useful field to study.

Nobody in my family had ever been to university but my father thought that sounded sensible so we made an appointment with the dean of the Vet School at Sydney University. Very important man. And we came down to the city to meet him.

Oh, beautiful Sydney University. Old classical buildings, very gracious. I was expecting to find out about the course, what I'd be doing, and where the classes would be. But, I was just ignored. Just him and Dad having a good old chat about the country and the weather, you know, the way men go on.

Finally my father got around to it—we've come to enroll young Marion.

The dean completely chopped him off. He just erupted—'What?! In my faculty?! Over my dead body!' They didn't have girls! Didn't teach women!

My father—politely as he could—asked: *why not?*

Well, the dean looked at my father, and huffed and puffed for an answer and finally he sputtered out—'Well, how would she throw an elephant?'

I'm not being metaphorical. That was his answer.

The interview was swiftly closed and we were ushered out the door.

Couldn't throw an elephant …

It makes no sense!

Slow it down, let all the pieces come apart. Observe …

How would she throw an elephant?

WOMAN 2: What did you say?

MARION BLACKWELL: Nothing. Wasn't allowed to speak.

WOMAN 5: What did you do?

MARION BLACKWELL: I just looked at him.

WOMAN 1: What did you think? Do you remember?

MARION BLACKWELL: Yes.

I thought: 'Are you an idiot?'

WOMAN 4: [*to audience*] There's a shape to the stillness and movement. What is moving, what is changing here?

MARION BLACKWELL: Until that moment, I had *never,* never ever dreamt that there was *any* reason why a girl shouldn't do *anything*.

I wasn't allowed to drive the tractor till my legs were long enough to reach the pedals. Those are the only sort of impediments that I remember.

But now, this changes: there's a Rule. Women aren't *allowed*.

WOMAN 3: [*to audience*] Something else here is standing still. Something has not changed.

MARION BLACKWELL: Me!

Of course not.

I had to accept it because that's just the way it was. But I didn't really accept it. It was COMPLETELY UNREASONABLE.

But what could one little girl do about it? [*Laughs.*]

Stops laughing.

Change it, later on.

I'm not a great woman for giving people advice but: if the front door won't open, go around the side.

4.

> PROJECTION: **Marion Blackwell applied to study Science at Sydney University and was accepted. She specialized in plant ecology and physiology and graduated with honours, at the top of her year.**
>
> **She was immediately appointed Lecturer in Mycology—**

MARION BLACKWELL: Mycology! The study of fungi—the basis of everything!

> PROJECTION: **At the University of Technology, Sydney, becoming one of the first women to teach science in an Australian university.**
>
> **In 1958 she moved with her young family to Western Australia.**

5.

MARION BLACKWELL: Oh Western Australia in 1958—it was like going back in time.

Very few women working in science. And they were all stuck inside doing lab work.

And just in general, there weren't many people out in the field. Big mining projects were just being pushed through with not a lot known back in Perth about the terrain, or what was growing there.

In the early sixties, the call went out for people to go out and do scientific surveys in the north of the state. So I put up my hand—I had to get back outside! And I got the job—because none of the men wanted to do it! Too hard. No maps.

Took about three days to get there, right to the end of the highway, then dirt roads, then no roads. That was the point.

Oh people were so surprised! A woman! Will she be all right?

Didn't camp in the camps. Got out on my own right away.

Very interesting.

I grew up in the mountains, in snow country.

This country—never seen anything like it.

The perfume! The smell of the eucalypts.

And the sky, the unrelenting West Australian sky.

You find extraordinary things. The most amazing plants out in the desert that have developed all sorts of clever adaptations to survive—much cleverer than cacti. Cacti just conserve water; these plants photosynthesize in the dark.

This country of ours is something quite special in the world. It is an amazing, ancient land. We've only just scratched the surface of understanding what can grow here, what's evolved and what's still unfolding.

After I did my first survey I was rung up and asked to do another and another because [*laughing*] they learnt that I could do it.

6.

MARION BLACKWELL: From the moment I got to Western Australia I'd been trying to find the honey pot mountains. I asked, I described them, but nobody knew anything. I went to the museum, to the university. Everyone said 'There is no record of any such thing, you must be dreaming.'

I knew I wasn't.

A long, long time afterwards I was out on survey in the Osmond Ranges in the Eastern Kimberly. I was coming back down through the valley onto the plain at dusk. And looking towards the sunset, there absolutely silhouetted on the skyline were these honey pot mountains.

I got back and said, 'Why isn't this place on the conservation reserves?' The response was—'Marion, nobody in Perth had any idea that they existed.'

Pause.

Aboriginal people have known and lived in this place for at least forty thousand years. It is Purnululu. The honey pot mountains are the Bungle Bungles.

PROJECTION: PANORAMIC IMAGE, rear and side walls.

The Bungle Bungles open out across the theatre.

PROJECTION: Purnululu was declared a National Park in 1987.

In 2003, the United Nations inscribed it on the World Heritage List as 'A site of outstanding universal value from the point of view of science …

representing major stages of earth's history …

superlative natural phenomena … exceptional natural beauty.'

Go round the side.

7.

MARION BLACKWELL: I'm ninety-one tomorrow. I'm still working.
    Some things have changed a lot. And some things haven't changed at all. Women still have to perform five times as well to even get a chance. Long way to go.
WOMAN 6: Will you tell me what you've learnt about time and growth? All my life I have been told—don't be so impatient, things will change, it's just a matter of TIME.

MARION BLACKWELL: Time's got nothing to do with growth, with *producing* growth.

WOMAN 6: So, what produces growth?

MARION BLACKWELL: Water. Light. Good soil. Growth will be to do with the wind. It will be to do with lodgment of seed in soil—not being blown away.

Time doesn't do any of the *work*. Growth occurs *during* time, not because of it.

Pause, rising sounds of the bush.

WOMAN 6: It doesn't sound like much stopped you. If anything stopped you.

MARION BLACKWELL: No. Not while I'm myself. I don't think it will.

PROJECTION: Image of young Marion Blackwell; image of adult Marion Blackwell.

ANNE ALY

Anne Aly performed by WOMAN 8.

1.

ANNE ALY: My second husband and I were watching the TV late one night when they broke for a news flash. In New York, a plane had been flown into the World Trade Centre. It was September 11 2001. I sat on the couch whispering to myself: 'Please, please, don't be Muslims.'

I went back to university and did my PhD, trying to understand. Nothing scared me more than the thought of my own sons falling prey to this. I spoke to survivors, to people who had lost someone, to men who had carried out terrorist attacks.

It was an unusual thing, at the time, for a Muslim woman to be speaking about it.

Why do these people carry out terrorist attacks?—I'd get asked. Well, what about the fact that *these people* are mostly *men*?

Pause.

At some level, it's gendered violence.

You can see it in the propaganda of all sorts of extremists—
it's very, very masculinized. Whether it's Jihadists or white
supremacists: on the surface, it's all about strength and power; but
underneath they're appealing to the same basic fear. The world
is changing. Men need to fight for their masculinity. Women are
entering the space men occupy.

Every time women impinge on men's territory, they get very
tetchy. Do you know why?

PROJECTION: Dr Anne Aly

Born 1967, Alexandria, Egypt

Counter Terrorism Expert

I wrote books and papers, I spoke at conferences, at the UN, in the
White House. And in 2015, I said to my current husband 'Nothing's
gonna change because there's no political will.'

Three days later, I got a phone call from the Australian Labor
Party.

My first response was, 'I've got a research program set up, I'm a
professor. Why would I do that?' And they said, 'Because it would
be a different way to make change.'

**PROJECTION: The lead-up to the 2016 Australian Federal
Election**

**Dr Anne Aly, Counter Terrorism Expert, announces
she will stand for the seat of Cowan in Perth's northern
suburbs.**

ANNE ALY: In politics, they love you to have a story.
        Woman. Single mother. Muslim. Professor.
ENSEMBLE: What a great story!

2.

WOMAN 1: Anne Aly was born in Egypt!
WOMAN 2: Her family came to Australia when she was two!
WOMAN 3: She grew up in the Western Suburbs of Sydney!
WOMAN 4: When she was little, she wanted to be a teacher!
ANNE ALY: The first thing I *really* wanted to be was—

Eerie music, weird lighting.

—a Paranormal Scientist.

One day I said to my mother: 'Mama, I think we are asleep. This world—it's not real, it's just us dreaming.'

Mum glared at me, 'Don't think too much. You go mad and no one marry you!'

She had this old Arab phrase:

PROJECTION [*Arabic*]: **'dul el ragal wala dul el heit'**

It sounds romantic, doesn't it? Wait till you hear what it means!

PROJECTION: 'The shade of a man is like the shade of a wall.'

Even then, I remember thinking so the man shields you from bad things but—is the man shielding you from good things too? That's what walls do.

[*Mother's voice*] 'Thinking! Thinking!'

So I respected it, and at the same time, I really wanted to rebel against it.

I grew up into two different versions of myself: a dutiful Egyptian daughter who studied hard and got good grades. And inside, a budding feminist questioning everything.

When I finished school all my hard work paid off and I earned a place at Sydney University studying law—my first choice. But by then …

My sister had set the example by marrying, and I was expected to follow—get married and take my place in the shadows.

PROJECTION [*big*]: **Anne Aly wedding photo.**

3.

ANNE ALY: I threw myself into my newfound role as Betty Baker Perfect Homemaker.

I guess, when you look back, you see things that you didn't see at the time, signs I should have picked, but I brushed them off …

One time, when our son Adam was about six months old, my husband came home and I'd made fish for dinner. I hadn't had time to cook some big elaborate meal. And he was angry at me. He didn't get how hard it is to be with a baby all day.

Breaking from the story to give a kind of impromptu speech.

We still haven't come to grips with that in this country. No. That's *labour*. If it was easy, day care centres would be full of men making a hundred grand a year, not women, making twenty grand a year.

... One of the many things I was going into politics to change ...

Back to the story.

Anyway, that night, my husband got really angry about the fish for dinner.

The end of that story.

Years later, long after I'd left him, I was at a forum for International Women's Day. I never prepare speeches. I was handed the microphone and I looked out at all these women and girls—

There was one part of my story I'd never talked about ...

Beginning new speech.

We'd been married a few years, Adam was about eighteen months old, the first time my husband hit me.

Pause.

He hadn't come home for two days, and when he finally showed up, I said, 'Where were you?' I stood up to him. So he hit me.

It didn't make me cower. It made me angrier.

I got up and said, 'Is that all you've got?'

And he hit me again.

Stand up, take some more. Stand up, take some more, until I couldn't take any more.

Pause.

I went to court to get a restraining order.

The judge said—'The police will come to your house and take your husband away in front of your son. Is that what you want?'

I was a twenty-something mother with a toddler to care for.

I stayed. Like lots of women stay, because I didn't think I had a choice.

I had another baby with him, my second son.

This was our marriage.

I understood that.

But I never accepted it.

It was an out-of-body experience.

Your husband sees you as property, and so you behave like property, even though you know that you are not property.

Inside, everything knows—this is wrong.

Pause.

It went on for years. In the end, I didn't leave because things blew up, actually they just got so small.

One night we all had flu. And he said, 'I'm going out.' I sat there waiting for him, with Adam and Karim asleep on me, and Adam wet himself and I couldn't move.

And I just thought, this is my life.

The three of us on this one chair ... sick, trying to sleep, *waiting for him.*

Pause.

And I thought, no. I'm out.

But the story wasn't finished.

I remarried.

And that husband too was abusive.

By now I was in my forties. A professional woman with a high paying career teaching counter-terrorism! I remember just going— What's wrong with me?

Until you finally go, hang on a minute, it's not me. It's them.

4.

Breaking off from the International Women's Day Speech. Sounds of phone ringing, text messages, email and twitter alerts start and continue to build throughout this scene.

ANNE ALY: After I told my story, a lot of women got in contact with me.

A lot.

Lawyers and doctors and teachers and all sorts of women who said, I went through that and there is so much shame talking about it—somehow you're so stupid, why did you stay in that relationship?

A lot of women from all sorts of ethnic backgrounds contacted me.

A lot of Arab women, who wanted to call this out within our communities.

The problem is—when we call it out, everyone else jumps on it—oh, those *Muslim* men!

Yes. It makes them feel better. I mean '*I'm* living with Western pornography and Western harassment, actually—I can't even catch public transport home late at night. But at least I don't have to wear the burqa!'

Woah, hang on! Save yourselves from your own men. I don't need you to save me from my religion.

Because this skin that I wear, and everything I've lived through inside this skin, are a skill and a resource and knowledge. They are powerful.

5.

ANNE ALY: Powerful enough that when I told my story, and caught so much shit from Muslim men—'Oh, you know we already suffer. Now we're going to be judged even further.' I did not back down. I said 'Oh, sorry you are being judged but—

ANNE ALY WITH WOMAN 6: women are *dying*.'

ANNE ALY: Powerful enough that when the Men's Rights Activists came after me …

And the death threats, the calls to—

PROJECTION: 'hang her from a tree'

'drown her in pig's blood'

'put a bullet in the bag'

WOMAN 5: Is that all you've got?

ANNE ALY: I did not back down. No no no. Let's take this apart, shall we?

It is ALL CONNECTED, isn't it?

It's about power and these men who think they own women, who think they own women's bodies. When did I—

WOMAN 4: —I didn't—

ANNE ALY: —give you permission to touch me, mate?

WOMAN 1: I can control *my* desire.

ANNE ALY: That's right.

WOMAN 2: I mean what makes you think your sexual engine is so much more powerful than mine?

ANNE ALY: It's not.

WOMAN 7: It's everywhere you go.

ANNE ALY: Being hit, for me, was just a physical manifestation of everything else in my life that says,

ANNE ALY WITH WOMAN 3: 'Sit down and shut up!!'

ANNE ALY: No safe way to talk about it, without being dismissed as just political correctness gone mad.

PROJECTION: **Politically correct, hysterical, angry, angry woman, feminazi, loony left, can't take the heat.**

[*In synch with projection*] Politically correct, hysterical, angry, angry woman, feminazi, loony left, can't take the heat—which is to say:

ENSEMBLE: SHUT UP.

ANNE ALY: [*quiet, nasty*] We don't want to hear it.

Pause. By now the beeps and alerts are continuous, and the sounds blur into one sound, which rises. ANNE ALY *and* ENSEMBLE *stop to hear it fully.*

But the second you can actually hear it from so many other women then it's a different picture. Like little dots—that connect to make a very different picture.

Yes, yes, it's all connected.

That's what I went into politics for.

6.

PROJECTION: **Canberra, 30 August 2016**

The 45th Australian Parliament convenes, with the first ever Muslim woman Member, taking her seat—Dr Anne Aly.

Reprise eerie music and lighting.

ANNE ALY: Canberra!

That first term in Parliament was a bit crazy, actually.

I was all kind of deer-in-the-headlights-idealistic about the things I was going to achieve.

Dear, oh dear.

I mean Parliament House itself is not necessarily a sexual harassment free environment.

It's not. Not at all.

A lot of staffers were very young women, you'd see them with their male boss, three, four, five of them,

ENSEMBLE *performs this.*

and he's walking along like he's King Muck and they're his little concubines. Extremely disturbing.

Julie Bishop used to walk through Parliament with an entourage of female staffers.

ENSEMBLE *turns on their heels and performs this too.*

You'd never see her with a male staffer. She'd have five female staffers, and they would march right on through like the mean girls in school. Like a fucking army.

So … okay, okay, first term, okay, I'm finding my feet.

Anne, trust how much you know, trust your expertise, how good you are at your work, let's do that.

By the time I've won a second term—I'm ready to get going.

I want to work in National Security—I have a PhD in Counter Terrorism.

If you're a man with a PhD, you get put on the committees that use your expertise. If you're a woman with a PhD, it's like you did your PhD as a fucking hobby, you know?

I want to work in domestic violence. Does anyone ask me what we should be doing about domestic violence? Because—I can tell you.

And it's not because I've researched it or anything—even though I have, and it's not because I wrote a book about it—even though I have, and it's not because I did a major report on it—even though I have. It's because I've lived it.

Every time women impinge on men's territory.

They get tetchy.

Do you want to know *why?*

[*Shouting at the audience—we'll need a yes*] DO YOU WANT TO KNOW WHY?

Because they're afraid we're better than them.
[*Laughing*] It's true.
[*Stops laughing*] It's true.
Parliament, as an institution, is *built* on patriarchy and racism.
But it's not just in politics, it's everywhere.
'Come, come. Sit at the table with us.'
Yeah, and be quiet.

Pause.

7.

WOMAN 2: What are you going to do?
ANNE ALY: I don't know.

Long pause.

WOMAN 5: You're a strategist—
ANNE ALY: Yes. I am.

Long pause.

WOMAN 6: This is the moment we have to show up for. We thought it was fixed—
ANNE ALY: [*quietly*] It's not fixed, it's fucked.

We showed up to be parliamentarians. We showed up to be vets, or priests or bar tenders. We want to do OUR WORK. So, what do I do now—because I actually can't do my work.

Right now, I have a choice.

Sacrifice any aspiration to do the things that made me say yes in the first place. And dedicate myself to being the fucking shit kicker and the disrupter so it's easier for the next woman and the next woman of colour.

Pause.

I say I have a choice, but … I really don't have a choice.

[*Starting to build*] Every time someone says to me, 'That's just the way it is' …

You know how many fucking times in my life people have told me 'That's just the way it is'? If I had accepted that, you know where I'd be now?

I'd still be in a violent marriage.
[*Crossing a line*] Don't fucking tell me that's just the way it is.
If that's the way it is, then the way it is needs to change.
[*Drawing it from the audience and herself—the absolute truth*]
IT'S NOT FIXED IT'S FUCKED.
I'm going to fix it.
Get out of my way.

PROJECTION: Image of young Anne Aly, and image of adult Anne Aly.

EPILOGUE: THE PERSISTENCE OF DREAMS

Eerie lighting and strange music—in softer hues and slower dreamy tones.

ANNE ALY'S MOTHER: [*voiceover*] Anne, Anne, stop thinking! You go mad. Nobody marry you.
ANNE ALY: I can't stop thinking Mama …
ENSEMBLE: None of us can …
ANNE ALY'S MOTHER: [*voiceover*] Thinking thinking!
ANNE ALY: Mama I think this world—it's us dreaming. We are just dreams.
WOMAN 4: I dream I'm six years old, and I'm running out to play halfback for Manly
running so fast
across the field
across time
until
I'm a grown woman sitting high in the stands.
Down on the field
the halfback catches the ball, and runs
her blonde hair streaming
my face streaming
with tears
for all the lost dreams
and the day they will find us.
WOMAN 5: I dream I am standing waist deep
in a sea

of six-year-old girls.

Each has her own story of the seas she has swum to find me.

And they tell me, all of them:

ENSEMBLE: [*to* WOMAN 5, *whispered, excited*] One day I will be the prime minister.

WOMAN 5: They are right. I feel it, on my skin.

I am standing in a sea of prime ministers.

WOMAN 1: I dream I am offered a new and very demanding job, complex, important work … I cannot quite recall what it is. Perhaps I am—

WOMAN 5: The prime minister

WOMAN 4: The world champion

WOMAN 3: A preacher of the word of God

WOMAN 1: Perhaps.

The job requires fine skills and judgements

And in my dream

I suddenly realise—

it is not really me who has been appointed to this work,

it is

my breasts

my wonderfully Large Breasts

and just as I am asking how they will ever manage, I become aware that my breasts are *thinking*—

WOMAN 2: —all our lives, we have been looked at, and spoken of, and never replied.

WOMAN 1: Now at last, they speak. They say …

WOMAN 3: We have dreamt of this space you offer us,

WOMAN 2: We are more than enough to fill it.

Pause, new beat.

WOMAN 3: [*looking to* WOMAN 2] *We* are not entirely convinced we are dreaming,

WOMAN 2: [*looking to* WOMAN 3] for we have never ceased to be awake.

WOMAN 3: [*to audience*] We have formed a group!

WOMAN 2: [*to audience*] We will pool our money to buy cigarettes and we're going to tell each other *everything*.

WOMAN 3: [*laughing*] You think you're going to shock me.

But I tell you—*Whither thou goest, I will go* ...

And you will lead me to where I am and have always been:

WOMAN 2 & 3: [*to each other*] I'm with her.

WOMAN 6: I dream I am six years old and I have emptied the library, I am sitting in a sea of books that stretches further by the second, my mother and my grandmother, their mothers and their grandmothers are handing me books,

and I will read every one and one day write my own too

I do not look up when I hear the sound of

footsteps

women and girls,

coming through the bushes, or sliding under the fence or climbing over the wall,

showing up.

To sit.

To listen.

To watch my mother and my grandmother, their mothers and their grandmothers pass the books on, one by one.

Streaks of ochre on my fingers from the pages.

WOMAN 7: I dream I'm six years old.

I'm looking for honey.

Crossing the creek, climbing the bank fast through the bushes

And I push through the undergrowth

And there—blocking my way—she is. At last.

The elephant.

Here.

Asleep, across the path.

So big.

And I am so little.

My feet won't reach the pedals of the car.

But with all the strength of the things I will see and know in my long, long life, I bend,

And pick her up.

She's *light*, like a feather.

Like a *feather:* destined for the air.

What a waste it would be to throw this elephant.

No, no.

Float her, just above the wing of the buzzing bee.
And watch for the up-light. She will point us to the honey.
Marvellous.
That way—

Pointing straight at the audience.

It's there.

THE END

Sources

PAM BURRIDGE

No Australian woman has won the pro world title
The first *amateur* world surfing championships were held at Manly in 1964. The women's world champion was Australian Phylliss O'Donnell

I know many people will be surprised to discover
Pam Burridge interview with *Sydney Morning Herald*, quoted p148 of *Pam Burridge* by Marion K. Stell, Angus & Robertson 1992

JULIA GILLARD

Thanks to Julia Gillard for permission to use her words from her writings, speeches and interviews.

I will not be lectured about sexism and misogyny by this man …
Hansard, Australian Parliament House, 9 October 2012

Ditch the Witch, Bob Brown's bitch …
'Anti-carbon tax rally attacks get personal' ABC Radio, PM 23 March 2011

Deliberately Barren …
'Heffernan targets "barren" Gillard', *The Bulletin*, 5 May 2007

Non-productive old cow …
'CEO compares PM to an old cow', *Sydney Morning Herald*, 4 August 2012

Small breasts, huge thighs …
'Julia Gillard's "small breasts" served up on Liberal party dinner menu', *The Guardian*, 12 June 2013

Yes. I do marvel at it …
'Julia Gillard's Global Warming: Life after Politics', Jacqueline Maley, *Good Weekend*, 13 July 2019

I used to love going to schools …
Launch of the Global Institute for Women's Leadership: Julia Gillard in conversation with Stephen Sackur, 5 April 2018

I'm the sort of person who likes to have a feisty go
Q&A, ABC TV, May 2013

Then you know slowly the penny dropped
Launch of the Global Institute for Women's Leadership: Julia Gillard in conversation with Stephen Sackur, 5 April 2018

When I was at university, intellectually I understood the barriers for women
Launch of the Global Institute for Women's Leadership: Julia Gillard in conversation with Stephen Sackur, 5 April 2018

I didn't go into politics to make it kinder or gentler.
Julia Gillard interview with Hilary Harper, *Life Matters*, ABC Radio National, 13 January 2021

In the theatre of Question Time, I gave as good as I got.
Women and Leadership: Real Lives, Real Lessons, Julia Gillard and Ngozi Okonjo-Iweala. Random House, 2020

I thought we were the generation that everything was going to be different for …
Launch of the Global Institute for Women's Leadership: Julia Gillard in conversation with Stephen Sackur, 5 April 2018

My memories of that day are in fragments
My Story, Julia Gillard. Penguin, 2019

Red Hot
'Gillard gets Red Hot', *Sydney Morning Herald*, 9 July 2010

Realisation of the Great Feminist Dream
'Realisation of the Great Feminist Dream', Caroline Overington, *The Australian*, 24 June 2010

Is This How You Smash a Glass Ceiling
'Is This How You Smash a Glass Ceiling?', *New Matilda*, 24 June 2010

It's a GIRL
'It's a GIRL', Catherine Deveney, Blog, 25 June 2010

I knew there'd be a lot of attention around it
Julia Gillard interview with Richard Glover, ABC Radio, 13 July 2020

The day after I became prime minister, I visited a shopping centre
Julia Gillard interview with Hilary Harper, *Life Matters*, ABC Radio National, 13 January 2021

These gendered references were going to just swirl around
My Story, Julia Gillard. Penguin, 2019

But in the hard political contests
Women and Leadership: Real Lives, Real Lessons, Julia Gillard and Ngozi Okonjo-Iweala. Random House, 2020

Anyone who chooses a life without children
'Anyone who chooses a life without children, as Gillard has, cannot have much love in them,' Mark Latham, *The Spectator Australia*, 5 Feb 2011

The longer I served as prime minister
Women and Leadership: Real Lives, Real Lessons, Julia Gillard and Ngozi Okonjo-Iweala. Random House, 2020

Threats of violent abuse, of rape
Julia Gillard speech In Memory of Jo Cox, 10 October 2016

I mean, there were moments when I felt the weight of it …
'Julia Gillard's Global Warming: Life after Politics', Jacqueline Maley, *Good Weekend*, 13 July 2019

Everyone likes to be liked
Launch of the Global Institute for Women's Leadership: Julia Gillard in conversation with Stephen Sackur, 5 April 2018

If a woman bites her tongue for too long
My Story, Julia Gillard. Penguin, 2019

Over many years, I'd honed the skills of dominating Parliament
Julia Gillard interview with Richard Glover, ABC Radio, 13 July 2020

For fuck's sake!
'On the Road with Julia Gillard', Chloe Harper, *The Monthly*, August 2013

Once I started, it just got a life of its own
In Conversation with Anne Summers, ABC TV, 2018

I meant every word of it.
Julia Gillard on 'A Podcast of One's Own with Sandi Toksvig', 12 June 2019

I didn't feel heated or angry
My Story, Julia Gillard. Penguin, 2019

Australian Politician Shrinks
'Australian Politician Shrinks in Embarrassment, as Prime Minister Destroys him for being a Misogynist', Joe Weisenthal, *Business Insider*, 9 October 2012

Best Thing You'll See All Day
'Best Thing You'll See All Day: Australia's Female Prime Minister Rips Misogynist a New One', Tracey Egan Morrissey, *Jezebel.com*, 10 September 2012

One badass motherfucker
'Australia's prime minister Julia Gillard is one badass motherfucker', Tracey Egan Morrissey, *Jezebel.com*, 10 September 2012

Yes. I puzzle at it still.
'Julia Gillard's Global Warming: Life after Politics', Jacqueline Maley, *Good Weekend*, 13 July 2019

For me, this had to be more than an intellectual journey
Women and Leadership: Real Lives, Real Lessons, Julia Gillard and Ngozi Okonjo-Iweala. Random House, 2020

Feminism has always come in waves
International Women's Day address at the Royal Women's Hospital, 8 March 2018

Early and hard
Launch of the Global Institute for Women's Leadership: Julia Gillard in conversation with Stephen Sackur, 5 April 2018

MARCIA LANGTON

One in six Australian women has experienced physical or sexual violence by a current or former intimate partner.
Australian Institute of Health and Welfare (16 Sept 2021), citing the most recent Australian Bureau of Statistics Personal Safety Survey, 2016

On average, one Australian woman a week is murdered by her current or former partner.
'A woman is still being killed each week in Australia', *The Guardian*, 1 March 2021, also Bryant, W. & Bricknall, S. (2017). *Homicide in Australia 2012-2014: National Homicide Monitoring Program report*. Canberra: Australian Institute of Criminology, 2017

Indigenous women are 11 times more likely to die due to assault than other Australian women.
Australian Human Rights Commission *Wiyi Yani U Thangani (Women's Voices): Securing Our Rights, Securing Our Future* report, 2020, Chapter 2.2[c] Experiences of Inequality—Law and Justice — Figure 2:16

Indigenous women are 32 times more likely to be hospitalized due to family violence.
Australian Human Rights Commission *Wiyi Yani U Thangani (Women's Voices): Securing Our Rights, Securing Our Future* report, 2020, Chapter 2.2[c] Experiences of Inequality—Law and Justice — Figure 2:16

In the Northern Territory, it's been estimated that Indigenous women are 80 times more likely to be hospitalised as a result of assault
Office of the Children's Commissioner *NT Cross Sector Induction and Orientation*, Alice Springs, 27 March 2014

Thanks to Marcia Langton for permission to use her words from the following sources:

There's a saying I learnt in my twenties
Marcia Langton interview with Shaun Carney, *The Mandarin*, 11 February 2019

The question most Australians will not ask is:
'Two Victims, No Justice', Marcia Langton, *The Monthly*, July 2016

I was called a crazy radical
Marcia Langton interview with Shaun Carney, *The Mandarin*, 11 February 2019

I tried to find a white-feminist defence of Aboriginal women
'For Her, We Must', Marcia Langton, *Griffith Review*, 2018 (Edition 60)

MARION BLACKWELL

Additional source, with permission of Marion Blackwell and the ABC:

Wisdom Interviews: Marion Blackwell on *Big Ideas* with Peter Thompson, ABC Radio National, 18 May 2003

ANNE ALY

Additional sources, with permission of Anne Aly:

Finding My Place, Anne Aly, ABC Books, 2018

Anne Aly, Emily's List Oration, 2016

Biographies

NIKKI KEATING

Nikki Keating has worked in hospitality for a decade in bartending and manager roles. She is a Communications Specialist based in Naarm (Melbourne). Originally from Queensland, Keating worked in journalism and communications until 2017 when she began working with United Voice and Hospo Voice. Keating was the face of the Respect is the Rule Campaign from 2017 to 2019, campaigning for zero tolerance policies in hospitality venues to help fight sexualised violence. In 2020 she co-founded The Consent Blueprints with psychologist, Ishma Alvi. The Consent Blueprints is a consent education and consultancy service. In 2020 they won a grant to build a program to help venues manage the risk of sexual harassment in hospitality and are currently working to get the course nationally accredited. Photo: Lucie McGough.

JULIE BATES AO

Julie Bates AO is the Principal of Urban Realists Planning and Health Consultants. She is also an 'out' sex worker and has been a harm reduction advocate and sex worker rights defender for more than half her life. She was a foundation member of the Australian Prostitutes Collective, the forerunner of SWOP, the NSW Users & AIDS Association (NUAA). She served on the Australian National Council on AIDS, contributed to the first Australian National HIV/AIDS Strategy and was a consultant to the World Health Organisation (WHO) on minimizing HIV risk in the sex industry. She was the inaugural sex industry liaison officer appointed to local government following decriminalisation of sex work in NSW. Today, she is a public speaker and lobbyist for decriminalisation of the sex industry and co-author and investigator on a number of sex work-related research projects including the pivotal multi-state UNSW Kirby Institute and Curtin University Law and Sexual Health Projects (LASH). Since the earliest days of the HIV pandemic and in a legal environment that still criminalised most aspects of the sex industry, Julie personally confronted some of the biggest brothel owners in Sydney with the reality that, in the context of HIV transmission, their businesses would continue to suffer unless they adopted a safe sex attitude and practice. Today she is a public speaker and political lobbyist for the decriminalisation of sex work and social researcher investigating harms associated with the various legislative and regulatory responses to sex work in Australia along with town planning and work health and safety advice to the sex industry and other key players. In 2018 she was awarded an Order of Australia. Photo: Walter Maurice, Urban Village.

TRISH MADIGAN AO

As a Catholic Sister for more than 30 years, and after time teaching in secondary schools and in chaplaincy work, Patricia Madigan is a prominent leader in ecumenical and interfaith relations in the Catholic Church in Sydney. She was a founding member of the Women's Interfaith Network. She completed her PhD at the University of Sydney in 2008 which was published as 'Women and Fundamentalism in Islam and Catholicism: Negotiating Modernity in a Globalised World' (Oxford: Peter Lang 2011). Trish is a member of the Congregation of Dominican Sisters of Eastern Australia and the Solomon Islands.

PAM BURRDIGE

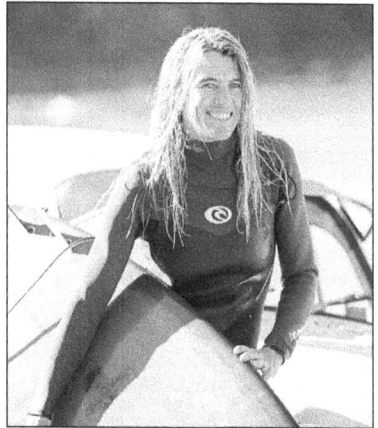

Pam Burridge was the first woman in Australia to become a full time professional surfer. Born in Sydney in 1965, Pam was given her first surfboard at the age of ten, she entered her first surfing contest in 1977 and took out first place. She continued her thirst for competition by entering and winning various amateur titles including the Australian championship which then led her to join the professional tour at the age of fifteen. By the age of seventeen she had her first runner-up finish, a result that would test her faith and patience another five times throughout her career. In 1990 she finally broke through winning the World Championship at Sunset Beach, Hawaii. Pam left the pro tour in 1998, retiring to the beautiful NSW South Coast where she coaches and runs a busy surf school and surf retreat business, with many girls and older women coming to her classes.

Hon JULIA GILLARD AC

Julia Gillard was sworn in as the 27th prime minister of Australia on 24 June 2010 and served in that office until June 2013. As prime minister and in her previous role as deputy prime minister, Ms Gillard was central to the successful management of Australia's economy during the Global Financial Crisis. Ms Gillard delivered nation-changing policies including reforming Australian education at every level from early childhood to university education, creating an emissions trading scheme, improving the provision and sustainability of health care, aged care and dental care, commencing the nation's first ever national scheme to care for people with disabilities and restructuring the telecommunications sector as well as building the National Broadband Network. Ms Gillard is the first woman to ever serve as Australia's prime minister or deputy prime minister. In October 2012, Ms Gillard received worldwide attention for her speech in Parliament on the treatment of women in professional and public life. In 2014, Ms Gillard was appointed Chair of the Global Partnership for Education. She also serves as Patron of the Campaign for Female Education and is Chair of Beyond Blue. In 2018, she was appointed Inaugural Chair of the Global Institute for Women's Leadership at Kings College, London. She is a Distinguished Fellow with the Center for Universal Education at the Brookings Institution in Washington, an Honorary Professor at the University of Adelaide, and is Patron of the John Curtin

Prime Ministerial Library in Perth, Western Australia. Ms Gillard has published two books: *My Story* and *Women and Leadership: Real Lives, Real Lessons*, which she co-authored with Ngozi Okonjo-Iweala. In 2017, Ms Gillard was awarded a Companion of the Order of Australia. Photo: Angela Wylie, *The Sydney Morning Herald*.

MARCIA LANGTON AO

Marcia Langton: I was born in Brisbane and at birth was Marcia Lynne Waddy, daughter of Kathleen Muriel Waddy, who later married Douglas Boyd Langton, a returned soldier who served in the Korean campaign. We moved from town to town, and I attended nine schools in all, such as one in southwest Queensland in the range of my grandmother's country where she and other relations had worked in the pastoral industry. My grandmother and grandfather, Ruby and Fred Waddy, were Bidjara and Iman (Yiman) respectively. My love of books and reading began in these country towns in the local libraries where I found peace and quiet. When my stepfather left, we moved to Brisbane. Not without a struggle, I attended the Aspley State High School, the University of Queensland, and much later after travelling overseas, the Australian National University and Macquarie University. I have a B.A. Honours, a PhD and D. Litt. And have managed to retain my driver's licence since obtaining it more than 40 years ago. I have been an academic since 1992 and written for both academic and non-academic audiences, advised on television programs and scripts, and appeared on radio and television shows as a commentator. Photos: Marcia Langton, 1982 by Juno Gemes, National Portrait Gallery, Australia © Juno Gemes/ Copyright Agency, 2022; Tom Hunt-Smith.

Dr MARION BLACKWELL AM

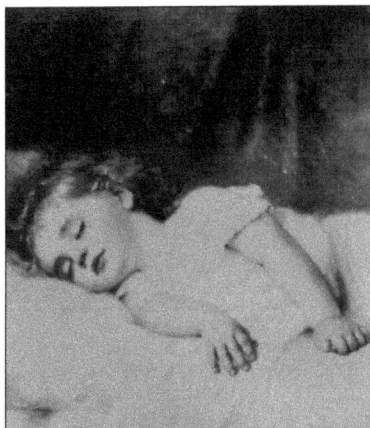

Marion Blackwell is an Environmental Scientist and Landscape Architect. She was born in 1928 on a sheep and cattle station, high in The Great Dividing Range, near the Queensland border. Her early education was through Blackfriar's Correspondence School (later, School of the Air). Graduating in Science from Sydney University in 1952, majoring in Plant Ecology and Physiology, she was immediately appointed lecturer in Mycology at the at the University of Technology, (now the University of NSW); a position she held until moving to Western Australia with her husband and young family in 1958.

She has continued lecturing part-time at the University of Western Australia in the Department of Botany and in the School of Architecture, Landscape and Visual Arts. Meanwhile she established her own Landscape Architecture practice, carrying out a broad spectrum of consultancy work in the fields of ecological and heritage surveys (including details of native fauna, flora and vegetation), landscape assessments, feasibility studies, landscape design and site rehabilitation works. These have ranged through the vernacular landscape planning and design of new 'outback' mining towns for the arid north-west and inland deserts of Western Australia, to the establishment of a naval base, university campuses, botanical gardens, city squares, urban parks, roof gardens and indoor atriums. In her design work, Marion endeavors to find solutions that are appropriate to both the local ecology and the individual client and user needs; believing that good design can, in the fulfillment of functional requirements, establish an aesthetically pleasing, self-sustaining and comfortable human environment.

ANNE ALY

Dr Anne Aly was elected as the Federal Member for Cowan in 2016. Born in Egypt, Anne and her family moved to Australia when she was two years old. By her late twenties, Anne was a single working mother of two young boys in Perth. Anne went on to study her Masters and PhD at Edith Cowan University and held a number of senior positions within the WA Public Service. She then worked at both Curtin University and Edith Cowan University with a focus on counter terrorism and countering violent extremism. Anne has been an advisor to the United Nations Counter-Terrorism Directorate, and was the only Australian invited to address President Obama's Countering Violent Extremism summit at the White House. Anne is also the Founding Chair of People against Violent Extremism (PaVE), a not for profit organisation focused on empowering communities to challenge violent extremism.

FRANCESCA SMITH, dramaturg

Francesca Smith has a reputation as one of Australia's leading dramaturgs, with a specific and unique approach to the development of new work. She works with individual artists and theatre companies all around the country, has participated creatively in many playwrights conferences, been a mentor for ATYP, artistic director of Playworks, keynote speaker at JUTE Regional Theatremakers Conference, resident teacher for the NIDA Playwrights Studio and a judge for the Max Afford, Patrick White and NSW Premiers Literary awards. She has collaborated on many highly acclaimed projects and is currently working on a book about the delicate art of safely guiding new works to the stage.

VICTORIA MIDWINTER PITT, playwright

Victoria Midwinter Pitt is an award-winning documentary filmmaker, playwright and director. Victoria's documentary film practice has been in complex historical moments told directly, and only, by the people who have actually lived through them. Her films include *Frontier*; *Rampant—How a City Stopped a Plague*; *Surviving Mumbai*; *Leaky Boat* and *Afghanistan—Inside Australia's War*. Victoria's work has won Australia's major documentary awards including Walkley, AACTA, SPAA, and the NSW Premier's History Prize, and been nominated for two Emmys as well as Queensland and NSW premier's literary awards, AWGIE, Logie and UN Media Peace Prizes. Her films have screened at the UN and across the world's major film festivals and broadcasters. Victoria trained in theatre at London's Royal Central School of Speech and Drama. Her first play (based on her own anarchic coming out story) opened Spain's independent theatre festival the Alternativa at the Teatro Sala Triangulo in Madrid—*All the Things I Would NEVER Tell You In 8 Songs & 12 Pictures*. *I'm With Her* draws together all these rich threads of experience in the power and revelation of first-hand storytelling. Photo: Angelita Bonetti.